D1295699

# ALL THAT'S NOT FIT
# TO PRINT

techniques and tools for checking out content sourced online. Most importantly, this book places our current situation in a wider historical context. As humans, we've always been drawn to rumors and conspiracies, but how can we cope when digital technologies have supercharged everything, from the creation to the dissemination of false and misleading information? This book shows you how.

—Claire Wardle, PhD, Executive Director,
First Draft

*All That's Not Fit To Print* is an important and timely resource for information professionals grappling with issues of veracity, authenticity, and authority. It dives deep into current trends to inform the discussion and lays out actionable insights on how we should engage around questionable content.

—John Chrastka, Executive Director,
EveryLibrary

This timely clarion call to arms encourages librarians to be at the forefront of the fake news cultural and political battle, helping them to recognize their evolving roles in today's ethical and technological struggle and to be prepared to fight for the truth.

—Linda Landis Andrews, Director of Internships,
Department of English, University of Illinois at
Chicago

Amy Affelt, in *All That's Not Fit To Print*, has written an effective primer for librarians and information professionals on the challenge that is fake news. Covering the current development of this across social media, she covers the key issues, a variety of effective tools and resources, and an informed call for librarians to adequately arm themselves to combat the dreaded "fake news" scourge that we find ourselves in. Definitely worth a read for experienced and budding librarians.

—Hal Kirkwood, President, Special Libraries Association, 2019, and Bodleian Business Librarian, Sainsbury Library, Said Business School, University of Oxford

Amy Affelt's *All That's Not Fit To Print* is a timely, intensely interesting, and easy-to-read book full of important, commonsense advice for those of us in the library and information professions who want to hone our skillsets to become information quality experts. It is revolutionary in that it is a book to guide information professionals to realize their role and encourage growth of methods long present in our profession. Affelt's book is a must-read for anyone who wants to learn about information quality from one of the best in our field.

—Anne Craig, Senior Director, Consortium of Academic and Research Libraries in Illinois (CARLI)

Gone are the days when we could reasonably trust the news. As long as responsible journalism is under attack, we can no longer assume that news is grounded in facts and reality. Fortunately, Affelt provides the guidance we need to decide what to believe and what to discard.

—Kimberly Silk, Brightsail Research


With *All That's Not Fit To Print* author Amy Affelt gives us all that we need to identify and combat the fake news epidemic that is causing confidence in media to significantly decline. While aimed at libraries and librarians who are leading the way in developing digital and information literacy skills, this book's advice is for everyone who seeks to ensure that the information they use and share is of the highest quality. Kudos to Amy Affelt for producing a very readable, enjoyable, and easy to understand guide to separating distortions, misinformation, and lies from the high-quality information we need to make good decisions on a daily basis.

—Donna Scheeder, President, International Federation of Library Associations and Institutions (IFLA), 2015–2017, and President, Library Strategies International


Reasoned and passionate, thorough and provocative, Amy Affelt's latest does much more than recap the issues and name the disease: she's created a clear roadmap for librarians and media people alike to ensure reality-based reportage not only survives but flourishes.

—Brendan Howley, Library Advocacy Specialist, Media Software Designer and Former CBC TV Investigative Journalist

Informative, insightful, in-depth. Amy Affelt uses her expertise, as a noteworthy research librarian, to teach others about fake news and how to work the complex and convoluted process of obtaining accurate informational text. *All That's Not Fit To Print* is helpful, timely, and relevant.

—Angela Falter Thomas, PhD, Associate Professor of Literacy Education, Bowling Green State University

# ALL THAT'S NOT FIT TO PRINT: FAKE NEWS AND THE CALL TO ACTION FOR LIBRARIANS AND INFORMATION PROFESSIONALS

AMY AFFELT

United Kingdom – North America – Japan – India
Malaysia – China

Emerald Publishing Limited
Howard House, Wagon Lane, Bingley BD16 1WA, UK

First edition 2019

**British Library Cataloguing in Publication Data**
A catalogue record for this book is available from the British Library

ISBN: 978-1-78973-364-8 (Print)
ISBN: 978-1-78973-361-7 (Online)
ISBN: 978-1-78973-363-1 (Epub)

ISOQAR certified
Management System,
awarded to Emerald
for adherence to
Environmental
standard
ISO 14001:2004.

Certificate Number 1985
ISO 14001

INVESTOR IN PEOPLE

*For my husband, Michael G. Leslie, who is literally wearing it.*

# CONTENTS

# ACKNOWLEDGMENTS

Doris Helfer was the first mentor and colleague to approach me regarding the need to study the impact of fake news on librarianship. Since my initial presentation with Doris, many other colleagues have invited me to share my views as well as learn from theirs; thank you to John Bryans, Theresa Cramer, Jane Dysart, Kathleen Lehman, Marydee Ojala, and Sara Tompson.

Dr Toby Pearlstein is always incredibly generous with her time and expertise regarding all aspects of my work, and she was her usual supportive and encouraging self while I worked on this book.

I would also like to thank Margaret Pasulka Ritchey and Brigid Pasulka for their insight and guidance, and Brad Beeson for reasons known to him.

It is often said that the experience of being an only child is largely dependent upon who your parents are. Gerald Affelt and Carol Hughett Gugerty are the best parents anyone could ever hope to have, and I am beyond fortunate to be their one and only.

Finally, my husband, Michael G. Leslie, has taught me so much, in particular that the simple act of living can be such a joy. Thank you, Michael, for always believing that I can do so much more than I ever think possible.

# INTRODUCTION

For as long as I can remember, news has played a central role in my life. Every day of my childhood, I woke up to WLPO, the local AM radio station that broadcasted all of the overnight happenings of our community of 10,000 residents, to which my father listened while he prepared for work. If it were a summer day, I would then walk a few blocks northeast to my Grandma and Grandpa Affelt's home, where WLPO's popular program, *The Clearinghouse*, would be on. A kind of early precursor to Craigslist, *The Clearinghouse* featured local residents phoning in and trying to sell everything from a set of snow tires to a litter of kittens to any interested neighbors. Next, I traveled across the alley to my Grandmother Hughett's home, where she could be found on her patio with the previous night's local newspaper, *The News Tribune*, checking out the latest adventures in the *Brenda Starr* comic strip, and working the crossword puzzle. At the end of each day, my mother would read to me from *Chicago Tribune* columnists Mike Royko and Ann Landers, even though Chicago seemed as far away as Mars to a young girl growing up amid the cornfields of central Illinois.

It never occurred to any of us in our family or community that the news that we consumed on a daily basis was anything but, as a character on a popular television program of the time espoused, "just the facts, ma'am." We trusted the content in every story and report that we read. We believed the written word of the reporters and writers as if it were sacrosanct. Sure, there was occasional hyperbole, but it was easy to spot. Humor was relegated to sections labeled as such, and perhaps we were a bit naïve, but critical judgment regarding source was not a consideration. We were pedestrian consumers of information; we weren't considering it in a professional context. Although I didn't know it at the time, that was the work of librarians.

Evaluating information integrity and quality has always been part and parcel to the mission of librarianship. On a basic level, the library itself is a repository of content and information, and none of it is fake news. Patrons should be confident that if they consume their news from the library, they are receiving accurate content. However, the library is not the primary source of news or information for American consumers. A 2017 Pew Research Center study found that 67% of Americans get at least some of their news from social media, and they are getting it from multiple outlets; Pew found that 26% of American adults get their news from two or more social media sites (Shearer & Gottfried, 2017). In this brave new world, the role of the librarian is more important than ever before, not because we are no longer the main conduits of news content for consumers, but in spite of it. If our patrons are getting their news from social media, Google search results, and shares from "friends," they are definitely no longer looking to the library as the chief source of news content (if they ever did). Therefore, librarians need to be much more than providers of factual content. We need to help our requestors make critical choices regarding which news to consume. We need to ensure that they understand how to determine what is real and what is fake, and that process begins with our own training and continuing education regarding information veracity and quality and data sourcing and transparency.

Luckily, librarians are well poised to lead the fight against fake news, and indeed, we have already been tapped as the profession best able to determine the accuracy of information content. It was a proud librarian moment for me when Christiane Amanpour, CNN's chief international correspondent, used a graphic from the International Federation of Library Associations and Institutions (IFLA) in a segment on spotting fake news in February 2017 (IFLA Website, 2017). The IFLA infographic offers numerous red flags to look for when determining veracity of news, and Amanpour's endorsement lent credibility not only to IFLA's checklist but also to IFLA itself and its member librarians as guides through the landmines of misinformation. Indeed, the final admonishment in the list is "Ask an Expert," with a subtitle of "Ask a Librarian." If there were any doubt that this should be our mission, an endorsement from Christiane Amanpour should be all that we need in order to reinforce a role that we always knew that we had. However, even if we have worked in information literacy before, others may have been unaware of our specialized training in this area, so it is critically important that we market our skills and abilities in order to be seen as the go-to professionals for finding relevant information and data from high-quality sources. It may not seem like a new role to us, but it may be seen that way to others, so in that case, it is, in a way, a new role for librarians to assume. We also need to become and remain first and foremost in the minds of the decision-makers at the organizations in which we work, whether they are senior executives at corporations, partners at law firms, deans at universities, or boards of directors of public libraries.

Marketing is always tricky, and marketing ourselves as truth-tellers in an era of quick information that is accessed outside of our presence can seem daunting. However, the good news is that we already have the skills; we just need the promotional tools and self-confidence to make them known. Most of us took information literacy courses in library school and we practice their tenets on a daily basis. Determining which data and content are needed, finding that information from the most credible source, and accessing it, analyzing it, and packaging it in a way that resonates most clearly with our stakeholders are among the most basic activities of a reference librarian. We just need to be able to market the services that we currently provide within the landscape of a world of alternative facts and fake news. Our requestors are probably aware that we undertake these activities, but they might not make the connection that their importance takes on a new urgency in the current climate. Not sure how to get started? Think of the tagline, "Is This Real News? Only Librarians Know for Sure."

When we serve as purveyors of truth and position ourselves as the professionals best able to help others navigate fake news, we also expand our skill sets and open ourselves up to new career options. Not only do we practice the skills explained above and "lead by example" when working on reference projects, but also we are able to teach information literacy and best practices for evaluating information to others. Further, we are expert at judging the quality of the information retrieval systems themselves. While we have always worked with proprietary databases and have always understood which types of indexing and metadata form the components of a robust, effective search engine that returns relevant results, it is likely that others in our organizations do not have this same expertise.

The following elements of the "Competencies for Information Professionals" document from the Special Libraries Association (SLA) directly address skills that librarians can use in establishing themselves as experts in determining fake news (Special Libraries Association, 2016):

- Systematically evaluating new or unfamiliar resources by applying analytical frameworks and methods;
- Delivering authoritative information resources to meet the needs of a particular audience, cover a certain topic, field, or discipline, or serve a particular purpose;
- Teaching others to critically evaluate information and information sources;
- Critical thinking, including qualitative and quantitative reasoning;
- Assessing the veracity or quality of information and its underlying sources in search engines and information retrieval systems.

Imagine the damage to an organization if misinformation, bad data, and erroneous facts are used. In corporations and law firms, they can cause the loss of a client or case, but in hospitals and medical centers, they can literally be a matter of life and death. If we position ourselves as the professionals who can best help our requestors avoid worst-case scenarios and information and data disasters and are seen as expert in doing so, not only will we be seen as hugely important assets but also we can teach others in the organization about our best practices and the ways to avoid the pitfalls that could truly lead to an institution's downfall.

How can we do this? This book will show you how. Whether you are a public librarian assisting patrons who need to understand the real way that the Affordable Care Act works, a corporate librarian using data in order to land a client, close a deal, or market a product, a law firm librarian who needs to find precedential law for an attorney building a case, or an academic librarian assisting professors with research, this book explains best research practices, how to maintain them, and how to teach them to others.

Fake news can have many different meanings. It can be deliberately created with a goal of misleading, a result of shoddy research, satire accidentally taken seriously, or a combination of those scenarios along with many more. This book explains the different forms fake news can take and the motivations behind individuals who create this content. It reviews several different guiding documents for spotting fake news and outlines best practices for spotting fake news and assisting requestors in doing the same.

A large portion of this book is dedicated to how fake news spreads through social media. Social media is the major conduit for the dissemination of fake news and as of this writing, no all-encompassing, foolproof remedies have been devised. In explaining the various offered solutions, whether they were actually implemented or remain in beta, this book takes a look at the complexities of social media platforms and their advertiser-supported business models. Since shedding light on fake news does not generate revenue, social media platforms have no incentive to call it out. IT and technology thought leaders have offered solutions and visions for an ideal social media world; this book discusses these options and their feasibility. Finally, this book considers the future of information sources and content. What will the future of fake news look like? What new tools and skills will librarians and information professionals need to not only navigate but also lead in this brave new world?

This book is for you if you:

- find yourself wondering, "What is meant by the term 'fake news'? How did we get here?";
- are looking for tools to use in order to spot fake news;

- would like to learn how to teach others how to select quality sources and choose quality content and data;
- are a library and information science (LIS) student and want to learn about the challenges of dealing with fake news in the field;
- need to determine how to find quality text and data sources for basic reference requests;
- want to learn more about the fake news/social media relationship and potential remedies to the sharing of fake news;
- would like to learn how to market yourself and your skill set to your management in order to become an information quality expert in your organization;
- are curious about the future of fake news and how it will affect our work as librarians.

Students and journalists are already looking to librarians as the experts in determining fake news. Whether or not we have the desire to assume this role is largely up to us, but in a way, it isn't a choice, as we are already there. Whether you want to apply traditional research and reference skills to the brave new media landscape, and market yourself and your skills in order to become an information veracity expert, or just want to learn more about the current news climate and make sure you and your organization "get it right," this book is for you.

# 1

# FAKE NEWS: FALSE CONTENT IN A FAMILIAR FORMAT

"Dewey Defeats Truman." "Hillary Clinton Adopts Alien Baby." Whether it was an error in judgment in a rush to publish election results in November 1948, or a tabloid cover designed to insight an eye roll and a chuckle in June 1993, fake news has been around for a long time. In the case of "Dewey Defeats Truman," the *Chicago Daily Tribune* became caught in a "perfect storm" of mishaps; in the face of a printers' strike which forced them to go to press hours earlier than usual, they relied heavily on polls which showed Republican New York Governor Thomas Dewey besting US President Harry S. Truman. The result was arguably one of the most infamous newspaper headlines in history, and the subsequent photo of a jubilant President Truman holding the front page of the paper aloft is one of the most recognizable artifacts of twentieth century US political history (Jones, 2007).

When the *Weekly World News* ran the headline about Hillary Clinton's alien baby, it may have been intentional satire, but unfortunately, there were probably more than a few supermarket shoppers out there who saw the tabloid and thought, "If it weren't true, they wouldn't be able to print it." That attitude remains today, and it is just one of myriad beliefs that have led to the rise of creation and sharing of fake news. While fake news has always been out there, and critical judgment and thinking has always been required to separate the real from the fake, the rise of the Internet and social media has fueled the fire of fake news to the extent that erroneous content makes its way halfway around the world before we can even begin to consider its veracity. But the real damage lies in the repercussions of fake news going viral. What once required a next-day retraction or merely generated a good laugh has the propensity to seriously influence events such as the US presidential election.

What is fake news and when did it get here? Judging from mentions in the popular press, fake news became a "thing" around 2016. A search of all publications on Factiva from 1984 to 2015 results in around 12,000 documents that mention the phrase. A search from 2016 to mid-2018, however, uncovers over 160,000.

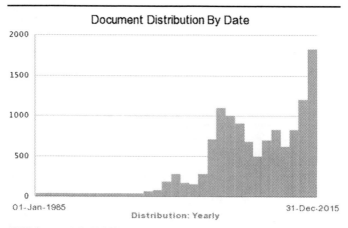

**12.2K documents for All Dates**

Source: Dow Jones Factiva.

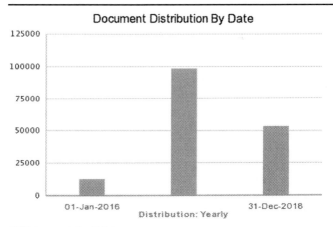

**Document Distribution By Date**

125000

100000

75000

50000

25000

0

01-Jan-2016        31-Dec-2018

Distribution: Yearly

**164K documents for All Dates**

*Source: Dow Jones Factiva.*

It is remarkable that in such a short period of time, the number of articles mentioning fake news has expanded so rapidly. Even more startling is a search looking for actual discussions of the concept of fake news. To find those, a search can be done for "fake news" in the headline or lead paragraph in all publications on Factiva. This results in around 3,000 articles from 1984 to 2015. In contrast, "fake news" in the headline or lead paragraph appears over 45,000 times from 2016 to June of 2018.

The difference in number of appearances in the press also represents a shift in the meaning of fake news. It can be argued that up until a few years ago (and in lockstep with the increase in article mentions beginning in 2016), the term "fake news" was used to describe outright falsehoods, or fabricated stories that are devoid of facts and totally wrong, regardless of agenda. Fast-forward to 2016 and beyond, and the meaning of fake news takes on a nuanced complexity.

Researchers at the Massachusetts Institute of Technology (MIT), who undertook the largest study of the phenomena to date, use the term "false news" rather than fake news in their research, stating that the term fake news "has lost all connection to the actual veracity of the information pre-sented, rendering it meaningless for use in academic classi-fication" (MIT Sloan School of Management, 2018). While it still may consist of completely erroneous information, and in some circles, it has become "an all-purpose insult for news coverage a person doesn't like," (Irwin, 2017) there are several different techniques by which content is fabricated or manipulated to masquerade as real news and is used to mislead.

Claire Wardle of FirstDraftNews.com analyzed the ecosystem of fake news and categorizes it by intention, dividing it into distinct content types (Michigan Library Research Guides, 2018):

- Fabricated content – content is 100% false and is "designed to deceive and do harm."
- Imposter content – fake news that lends the impression it is from a genuine source. An example of this is when a fake news story is written and the source listed is very similar to or even the same as a credible news outlet.
- Misleading content – using information to frame an indi-vidual or issue in a deceptive way.
- Manipulated content – taking credible information or visuals and changing them in order to deliberately mislead. We see this over and over again in posts and memes. A later chapter of this book discusses the use of manipulated con-tent to make fake videos.
- False context – manipulating credible information so that it is literally "taken out of context." There may be a kernel of truth within the content, but the details are unclear.

- False connection – "when headlines, visuals, or captions don't support the content." False connection is one of the most popular techniques by which "clickbait" sites drive traffic to websites and sell advertising. You may have seen a popular pop-up headline on credible news websites that reads similar to "(Insert B-List former celebrity name here) You Won't Believe What He/She Looks Like Now!" Of course we all are wondering what this person now looks like, so we click, and the owner of that ad is able to add one more tick to their tally of clicker-victims in order to command a higher price from their website client.
- Satire or parody – this content is meant to be humorous, but it can be easy to fall prey to it as real, especially when it is on a website whose other content is highly credible.

Wardle's categories fall under two umbrellas – misinformation and disinformation. While both can be considered fake news, their characteristics and intentions are very different. Misinformation is content that is mistakenly or inadvertently created; even though it is fake news, it is not written to intentionally deceive. One of the most common reasons why people share misinformation on social media is that they do not realize it is false and they believe it will be helpful to others (Wardle, 2018). Disinformation, however, is false content that is deliberately created to mislead people or to motivate them to adopt a certain viewpoint or agenda, obscuring the truth in the process.

The types of fake news that are created depend largely on the motivations of its authors. Why would someone want to create fake news? The path to understanding lies in the familiar admonishment, "follow the money." Many of these articles command a fee, regardless of content. It is also possible that they might be comedic and created by someone who just wants to entertain. Another theory is that they might be created by unethical reporters who are either under pressure and in a rush to be the first to publish a breaking news story, and in their haste, get the facts or the entire story wrong, or who feel the need to differentiate themselves from the plethora of Internet news sites by creating "unique" content that they have fabricated. Additionally, politics plays a role. Writing fake news is an easy way to stoke political fires and unite people behind a cause or candidate.

Finally, there is the system of "bots." Bots are basically computer programs that can be used to write false content which is then posted and shared automatically. Bots can also be used "to draw attention to misleading narratives, to hijack platforms' trending lists, and to create the illusion of public discussion and support" (Wardle, 2018). They can also be a part of a "botnet," which is a collective group of up to tens of thousands of other bots, acting in coordination but being operated by a single entity (Wardle, 2018). Botnets are the primary conduits of "manufactured amplification," which is the spread of information through artificial means. Manufactured amplification can be undertaken by several different methods including manipulation of search engine results, artificial bolstering of trending topics lists, and promotion of links and hashtags via social media (Wardle, 2018).

How did we arrive in this era of fake news? Again, in some ways, it is not new. In a TED talk in which he recommended 17 business books he thinks everyone should read, Bill Gates included 1954s *How To Lie With Statistics*, by Darrell Huff. The book "shows you how visuals can be used to exaggerate trends and give distorted comparisons," Gates said, calling it a "timely reminder, given how often infographics show up in your Facebook and Twitter feeds these days" (Baer & Lebowitz, 2015). To have Bill Gates describing a book written over 60 years ago as "timely" brings to mind the adage "Everything old is new again."

Huff's book explains that there are many different ways to "lie with statistics." His representations are not lies, per se, but rather, illustrations of the "false context" category. Basically, he shows how high-quality data from reliable sources can be manipulated to present certain viewpoints and possibly cause an audience to believe they represent exact facts, when in reality, multiple interpretations could be gleaned from the underlying data. One startling example in the book is the "Gee-Whiz Graph" (Huff, 1954). The Gee-Whiz graph is made by taking a basic line graph and slicing and dicing segments of the chart so that the line is more vertical because half of the chart is no longer there. For example, on a chart with representations of billions of dollars, if the amount being charted remains steady with an approximate 10% increase, the line looks fairly flat. If the increase is between 20 and 22 billion, and the chart begins with 0, the line again looks reasonably flat. If the bottom of the chart is lopped off, however, and the chart only shows between 18 and 24 billion, the rise looks much more substantial.

Just as graphics manipulation is not new today, Huff makes the point that it was not new in 1954. He writes that in 1938, an editorial in *Dun's Review* depicted the same government payroll data in two different line charts that look very dissimilar. Interestingly, one graph is labeled "Government Pay Rolls Up!" and the other is labeled "Government Pay Rolls Stable!" although the underlying data are exactly the same. A simple change to a more dramatic slope of the vertical axis on the chart can make flat federal employment appear to climb.

Fast forward to 2012, and selective depiction of data is alive and well. Naomi Robbins of *Forbes* noticed this phenomenon, taking issue with a bar chart displayed by Fox News (Robbins, 2012). The chart depicted then-presidential candidate Mitt Romney's interpretation of the top tax rates that would be paid if President Bush's tax cuts were allowed to expire. The chart begins with 34%, yet Robbins argues that all bar charts need to depict a zero baseline. A bar chart beginning one-third of the way to 100% serves as a modern-day example of "false context."

David Shere of Media Matters also wrote a blog post regarding this same misleading graphic; he created the below chart in order to depict the data in a more realistic illustration (Shere, 2012):

**Example: Zero Baseline Chart**

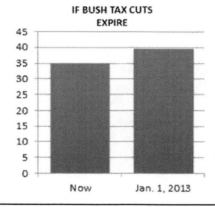

Fabricated content is what we typically think of when we hear the term "fake news." "Dewey Defeats Truman" and "Hillary Clinton Adopts Alien Baby" both fit into that category, even though the authors' intentions in writing those stories were very different; one was a poor judgment call in a rush to publish and the other remains a mystery. Sadly, the rush to judgment by the *Chicago Daily Tribune* wasn't the first and was hardly the last inadvertent error in the constant race in journalism by news outlets hoping to become the first outlet to report breaking news.

Journalists use the term "permanent exclusive" to describe situations where stories are published prior to their facts being verified (Thornburg, 2011). These occurrences have certainly happened prior to fake news entering the popular lexicon (*The Washington Post* documented many examples in great detail during the Iraq War in 2003) (Kurtz, 2003). In October 2017, *CBS News* was the source reporting the death of singer Tom Petty when he was still clinging to life in a Los Angeles hospital (CBS News, 2017a). While not really reporting fake news, CBS unfortunately had the "permanent exclusive"; that is, they were first but wrong. It was easy to fall prey to this report because a lot of us rely upon the old adage that had seemingly served us well up until this point: "consider the source."

Interestingly, one month prior to the CBS Tom Petty death mistake, PBS aired the 10-part Ken Burns documentary, *The Vietnam War*. In referencing archival news report footage, Burns relied heavily on CBS News, as *The CBS Evening News*, anchored by Walter Cronkite, known as "the most trusted man in America," (The Editors of Encyclopaedia Britannica, n.d.) shaped public opinion about the War and was largely responsible for it becoming known as "the living-room war" (Achenbach, 2018). After the Tet Offensive in January 1968, as the Viet Cong launched attacks through South Vietnam, Cronkite declared on-air that the war was unwinnable. President Lyndon Johnson, reinforcing Cronkite's authority and credibility, then told his staff, "If I've lost Cronkite, I've lost Middle America" (Achenbach, 2018). Some staff members even remarked that Johnson's decision not to run for reelection was a direct result of Cronkite's reporting. The Burns documentary, with its constant reminders of the importance of *CBS News*' reporting on the war, underscored *CBS News*' credibility at that time, and, it can be argued, that for a lot of us, that belief continued to the present day. Unfortunately, the Tom Petty bulletin, and its rush to report, served as a reminder that in a world where Twitter is "the new newswire," seemingly solid journalists are willing to take a chance when reporting information, in the hopes their facts are correct and they are the first to report a scoop. Whereas previously, news from credible sources could be taken as fact, we now need new standards for conducting research in this brave new world.

We have also seen reporters at highly credible sources publish fake news. ABC News, another mainstream source, suspended a reporter in December 2017, after he stated that former national security advisor Michael Flynn would testify that Donald Trump ordered him to contact Russian officials prior to the 2016 US presidential election (Wang, 2017). At the time, it was surprising that a veteran reporter would take such a chance, but again, in the hypercompetitive environment, merely reviewing the source of the content is not at all sufficient on its own in determining accuracy.

2017 also saw high-profile examples of completely fabricated content motivated by nefarious purposes. In the days immediately following the mass shooting in Las Vegas in October, it was reported that the perpetrator was an anti-Trump liberal whom the FBI linked to the Islamic State (Roose, 2017). This was later found to be untrue. In this case, however, the news outlet reporting that information was 4Chan, "a notoriously toxic online message board with a vocal far-right contingent," so it is highly unlikely that any trained librarians fell for that description.

Video is often used as the conduit for "imposter content" because it is easy to slice and dice from credible videos and create something new and false out of something older and credible. The results can be wide-reaching and extremely damaging. For example, following the school shooting in Parkland, Florida, in February 2018, a YouTube user with a screen name of "mike m.," took an old CBS Los Angeles affiliate video of an interview with massacre survivor David Hogg, and reloaded it with the caption "David Hogg The

Actor," implying that Mr Hogg, who had been speaking out against gun violence in the days following the shooting, was an actor hired by gun control activists in order to drum up support for their cause (Herrman, 2018). Eventually, You-Tube pulled the video for violating its anti-bullying and harassment policy, but not before it became a number-one trending video with over 200,000 views, generating comments such as "Someone get this kid an Oscar!" from the YouTube user community. Never mind the fact that the video was actually of Hogg commenting on a dispute with a lifeguard in Redondo Beach, California, in August of 2017 (in the video he mentioned that he was visiting the area); viewers saw Hogg on screen with the headline implying he was a victim for hire, and they became believers. YouTube had to deal with the fallout from the episode, even though the video's rise to popularity came from outside the YouTube community; link sharing on Facebook, Twitter, and conspiracy-theory websites caused it to go viral. Simultaneously, as Hogg appeared on CNN and stated, "I'm not a crisis actor, I'm not acting on anybody's behalf," the video continued to be posted and shared.

Graphics, images, and Internet videos are also the media of choice for manipulated content, and unfortunately, the consumer is often a victim of their own mind, as the manipulation causes the viewer to make assumptions without any underlying credible information. Photos on hardcopy magazine covers are an age-old example of this. Photoshopping and touch-ups have been around for a long time, and it is easy to conjure up an innate skepticism when viewing photos of models or celebrities, but consider the June 2018, *Time* magazine cover of a crying Honduran girl, superimposed next to an image of Donald Trump with a headline of "Welcome to America." It was easy to make the leap that she was taken from her parents, since the *Time* issue ran at the height of the debate over child/parent separation at US borders, but according to her father, the little girl was detained along with her mother at a facility in McAllen, Texas (Schmidt & Phillips, 2018); the photo was taken at the United States–Mexico border by John Moore of Getty Images as the little girl cried while her mother was patted down by a US border patrol agent. It is a heart-wrenching image to be sure, and the true circumstances of the actual photo are not easy to bear, but we need to look beyond what we see in order to find the facts. When we view an image, all of our life experiences and personal values shape our perception. In 1851, Henry David Thoreau wrote, "The question is not what you look at, but what you see" (Mis-Quotations, n.d.). His words are even more relevant today.

Misleading content can be characterized as "the type of fake news formerly known as false advertising." A Google search for the phrase turns up multiple articles regarding marketing in the first three pages of results, and as any insomniac can attest, late night television has been rife with misleading content since its inception. Those of us "of a certain age" might remember the old commercial with the Ginsu knife cutting through a tin can and then slicing a tomato in a demonstration of the Ginsu's ever-sharpness, or those pain medication spots featuring a hunky soap opera actor who stated, "I'm not a doctor but I play one on TV," in an effort to lend credibility to the product.

In the fake news realm, misleading content is rampant in health news articles. For example, a Google search for "effects of lemon juice on health" returns myriad examples of dubious health claims. The first page of results is rife with headlines such as "15 Benefits of Drinking Lemon Juice First Thing in the Morning," "9 Side Effects of Lemon Juice Overdose," "13 Impressive Health Benefits of Lemon Juice," etc., which link to articles stating that lemon juice can improve everything from asthma and diabetes to heart failure. Although some of the articles do contain links to underlying research, the connection between the findings of the studies and the tangible benefits stated in the articles are tenuous at best.

Clickbait has almost as many definitions as the reasons why we continue to fall for it, but in Wardle's groupings, it could be argued that it is almost synonymous with "false connection." The headline is the key to clickbait; as Ben Smith of BuzzFeed defines it, clickbait consists of articles that "do not deliver on the headline's promise" (Gardiner, 2015). Clickbait headlines rely on the emotions we feel when we read them. "Anger, anxiety, humor, excitement, inspiration, surprise – all of these are punchy emotions that clickbait headlines rely on," says Jonah Berger, who studies "social influence and contagion" at the University of Pennsylvania (Gardiner, 2015). And if curiosity kills the cat, it also fuels clickbait. At the peak of its popularity in 2013, Upworthy, "founded on a mission of promoting viral and uplifting content," had over 90 million unique visitors per month (Sanders, 2017). Upworthy relies on headlines ending in statements like "Here's what happened next," and "You won't believe it," and according to George Loewenstein of Carnegie Mellon University, the gap between what we know a little bit about and what we want to know more about motivates us to "obtain the missing information," and therefore click (Sanders, 2017).

Headlines with lists are also popular clickbait techniques. "15 Reasons," "9 Animals," – did you ever wonder why clickbait list articles often use odd numbers? The creators believe they stand out more prominently than even numbers when users are scrolling through feeds of headlines. Also, the numbers are usually not that large, which assures the reader that they will not have to devote a lot of time and attention to the content. Finally, they organize information spatially, and they indicate that there is an endpoint, giving us a sense of accomplishment when we finish reading the list. While it is true that many times, the text of a clickbait article is completely unrelated to the headline, once in a while it is spot-on, and as long as there is an occasional payout, our brains get a reward (dopamine), especially if the content is pleasing (i.e., 5 Cute Wombat Photos You Won't Want To Miss). Ironically, the fact that the payout isn't constant makes the times that the content is related all the more satisfying. According to Stanford neuroscientist Robert Sopolsky, when the reward frequency is only 50%, the anticipation that the content might be what you desire makes dopamine levels even higher when the reward is there. When we read a clickbait headline, we can never be sure if the text will be related. Sopolsky explains it this way: "you've just introduced the word 'maybe' into the equation, and maybe is addictive like nothing else out there" (Sanders, 2017).

When we hear the words "satire," "news," and "The Internet," *The Onion* is likely to come to mind. Founded in 1988 at the University of Wisconsin, Madison, *The Onion* is a parody of news that can sometimes seem so true that there have been instances of real news outlets citing *Onion* stories as sources (Wells, 2008). Not unlike *Saturday Night Live*'s "Weekend Update," it offers stories on current events with ironic and outrageous twists, written in a straightforward manner that mimics traditional news sites. Many other satirical news websites have attempted to do something similar; Kent State University has compiled a list of these sites, which they suggest that their students consult when they are unsure if a story they are looking at online is real (Kent State University Libraries, 2018).

It is possible, however, that an online story is satirical or meant to be taken tongue in cheek, and there isn't an obvious way to verify its content, and, according to Wardle, non-satirical but false content is sometimes labeled as satirical by its creators in order to evade fact-checkers (Wardle, 2018). A best practice is to check for a legal disclaimer on the website; it should state that the contents of the site are satirical. For example, *The Daily Currant* (http://dailycurrant.com/about/) states that it is a "satirical newspaper," and features a Q and A section declaring that all of its stories are "purely fictional." Another satirical news site on the Kent State list, NewsMutiny (http://www.newsmutiny.com/Index.html), has a banner across the top of its website that states "Satire for the wise. News for the dumb." That pretty much says it all.

# 2

# HOW WE GOT HERE

"A lie can travel halfway around the world while the truth is still putting on its shoes." That expression is commonly thought to have originated with Mark Twain, but ironically, the belief that Twain said it first traveled around the world many times before it was eventually revealed that it is actually a riff on a Jonathan Swift quote from 1710, "Falsehood flies, and the truth comes limping after it" (Chokshi, 2017). Regardless of which you favor, both expressions underscore the viral nature of fake news, and reinforce that again, its spread is not new, since Swift identified the concern in the eighteenth century.

Fil Menczer is an Indiana University professor who studies the spread of misinformation. Menczer's research has found that the lag time between the posting of a false news report and its subsequent debunking is around 13 hours (Solon, 2016). In other words, "enough time for a (false) story to be read by hundreds of thousands if not millions of people." Further, the fact that fake news is not always black and white, but instead largely consists of a "long tail of insidious half-truths and misleading interpretations that fall squarely in the gray area," allows people to create a narrative of their own. "People are more prone to accept false information and

ignore dissenting information," according to Walter Quattrociocchi, assistant professor of data science and complex
systems at the University of Venezia, Italy. Quattrociocchi
believes that his studies of the spread of false information have
reinforced the truth in the old adage, "We are just looking for
what we want to hear" (Solon, 2016).

Practitioners in other professions sometimes wonder why
librarians have a deep and overriding concern about fake
news. "It all comes out in the wash" is another folksy saying
that is sometimes used by people who do not share our
devotion to truth. Yet, information veracity is central to our
mission. On the first day of library school, we begin training
in information literacy, with a goal of becoming not only
proficient in its practice, but also in learning to teach these
practices to our constituents, regardless of the type of library
in which we work. According to the American Library
Association (ALA), information literacy is "a set of abilities
requiring individuals to 'recognize when information is
needed and have the ability to locate, evaluate, and use
effectively the needed information'" (The American Library
Association, n.d.). It encompasses a wide range of activities
and requires proficiency in several areas. According to ALA,
these competencies include the ability to:

- determine the extent of information needed;
- access the needed information effectively and efficiently;
- evaluate information and its sources critically;
- incorporate selected information into one's knowledge
  base;
- use information effectively to accomplish a specific purpose;
- understand the economic, legal, and social issues
  surrounding the use of information, and access and use
  information ethically and legally (The American Library
  Association, n.d.).

I often say that librarians show their love by clipping articles of interest and sending them to family and friends with a "read this and thought of you" message. This is a highly personalized activity; typically, we send an article to only one person. We are not participating in viral news sharing when we do this. Indeed, at first glance, the spread of fake news seems to be completely unrelated to sharing hand-selected single articles with friends. However, there are several commonalities and an underlying motivation that is quite similar. The process works like this: first, we see an article that garners our attention for some reason – we find it interesting, outrageous, relatable, etc. It might be connected to something else that we read recently, or maybe we were just discussing the same topic with friends. We want others to see it, so we share it, and if we do so using a social media platform like Facebook, it is easy to ignore the audience selector and share with all. All we would have had to do is skip one critical step – verifying that the article is from a credible source and that its underlying premise and statistics are based in fact and in sound research or science – and we have just spread fake news.

The sources that Americans use for news consumption play a large role in the spread of fake news. Pew Research Center found that two-thirds (67%) of Americans reported that they get "at least some of their news" on social media, with Facebook being the most common platform used (Shearer & Gottfried, 2017). This is impactful because "getting news" does not mean actually reading it. Previously, consumption of a news story might have been confirmed by the acknowledgment, "read it." In the current climate, "read it" is being replaced by "saw it," meaning that one saw and read the headline only. This theory was confirmed by computer scientists at Columbia University and the French National Institute, who found that six in 10 social media users share articles without clicking on them first. If 59% of links shared on social media were not clicked beyond the headline, "most people appear to retweet news without ever reading it" (Dewey, 2016).

The UK newspaper *The Independent* undertook a similar study and garnered results that were not only just as disturbing but also dangerous: they found that more than half of the 20 most-shared articles on Facebook in 2016 that had the word "cancer" in the headline were later discredited by either doctors, health authorities, or, as in the case of the most popular story, "Dandelion Weed Can Boost Your Immune System and Cure Cancer," by the source directly cited in the article (Forster, 2017). In many cases, readers of health-related headlines would not have needed to wait for the articles to be refuted. For example, *The Independent* identified the top five articles with HPV, or the human papilloma virus, in the headline and found that the three with the most "shares, likes, and engagements" were declared false by snopes.com, one of the oldest and largest fact-checking sites on the Internet. As social media becomes a go-to forum for health information, Dr Rachel Orritt of Cancer Research UK, has called for action, stating, "As Facebook is increasingly used as a news source, it's vital that incorrect articles are contested to prevent damaging health messages from spreading" (Forster, 2017).

In the days immediately following the 2016 US presidential election, fake news became the default rationale for election predictions gone horribly wrong. When Hillary Clinton lost to Donald J. Trump, pundits were left scratching their heads. Almost all of the major forecasting sites, from Nate Silver's FiveThirtyEight blog to the Princeton Election Consortium, put the probability of a Hillary Clinton victory at 70–99% (Lohr & Singer, 2016). Reasons for her defeat are long and varied, and it is widely believed that inaccurate polling data were a large part of the problem. The polling data used by the forecasting sites had several faulty characteristics:

- It didn't account for people who said they would vote but didn't.
- It didn't account for people who said they were voting for a particular candidate but changed their minds in the voting booth.
- It didn't account for people who did not want to admit that they were voting for a particular candidate.
- It didn't account for people who encountered long lines at the polling places and ultimately left without voting.
- It didn't account for people who registered to vote on Election Day, since the sample for most polls is "registered voters." Further, 1 of the 15 states that have same-day voter registration is Wisconsin, where polls leading up to the election had Hillary Clinton handily beating Donald Trump. It is speculative to assume that this option galvanized Trump supporters to register on Election Day, but it likely played a role, as Trump's margin of victory in Wisconsin was only 1%.
- "Caller ID, more than any other single factor, means that fewer Americans pick up the phone when a pollster calls," according to Dan Cassino in *Harvard Business Review* (Cassino, 2016). Caller ID limited the samples to those who either were unaware the caller was a pollster or were aware of it and wanted to be polled, making the samples less likely to be random, if potential respondents weren't answering the phone according to characteristics unmeasured by pollsters.

While the Monday-morning quarterbacking will probably continue for the next several election cycles, what is not open to debate is the notion that fake political stories ran rampant during that election and continue to do so today. Many of us are familiar with the quote, "If I were to run, I'd run as a Republican. They are the dumbest group of voters in the country. They believe anything on Fox News. I could lie and they'd still eat it up. I bet my numbers would be terrific," which has been widely attributed to a 1998 *People* magazine interview with Donald Trump. Many of us may be equally shocked to discover that Trump never said it (Solon, 2016). One more shock: the 20 top-performing fake news stories of the 2016 US presidential election were shared, reacted to, or commented on a staggering 8,711,000 times (Price, 2016).

And then there are the bots, which are ubiquitous and increasingly hard to detect. In an October 2017 *TechCrunch* article, a researcher behind the "Botometer" bot analysis tool estimated that 15% of Twitter users posting on political topic in the run-up to the 2016 presidential election were very likely not real people, but bots. Further, these bots were responsible for approximately 20% – or one in five – of political tweets appearing in the month prior to the election (Hatmaker, 2017).

Despite these alarming statistics, Brendan Nyhan, Professor of Government at Dartmouth College, believes their actual influence is minimal or nil. First, it is impossible to know how much of the shared content is actually seen. At the time of the election, only 21% of Americans were using Twitter (Greenwood, Perrin, & Duggan, 2016), and the percentage of voters using it declined in the voting populations with the highest turnout. For example, over 70% of Americans over age 65 years voted in the 2016 election, but only 8% of that age group were on Twitter (File, 2017). The percentage of voters declines as age lowers, with the largest group of Twitter users (with 40% using it) being ages

18–29 years (Statista, 2018). This group had the lowest voter turnout, at 46.1% (Greenwood, Perrin, & Duggan, 2016).

Also, voters who do use Facebook and Twitter need to be engaged with the platforms when the news scrolls. Further, Nyhan makes the point that people are often entrenched in their political views already and not easily persuadable. He and two colleagues, Andrew Guess of Princeton University and Jason Reifler of the University of Exeter, conducted a study which determined that fake political news exposure prior to the 2016 election was "heavily concentrated among a small group – almost 6 in 10 visits to fake news websites came from the 10% of people with the most conservative online information diets" (Guess, Nyhan, & Reifler, 2018).

Nyhan's findings indicate that fake political news is many miles wide and an inch deep, but it is still possible that fake news may have had some influence. David Rand, an associate professor of psychology, economics, and management at Yale University, did a study that found that Americans over age 60 years were more likely to visit a fake news site, with the odd finding that left-leaning voters were more likely to visit a pro-Trump fake news site than a pro-Clinton fake news site. Rand speculates that this could account for older, less-educated Obama voters switching to Trump in 2016, which he believes could have had an influence in states where the vote was close, such as Wisconsin (Carey, 2018). Also, there is the issue of turnout. It is highly likely that merely viewing inflammatory fake news galvanized voters who, up until the time of reading the fake stories, were unlikely to go to the polls.

A December 2016 Pew Research Center survey found that two in three US adults (64%) believe that fake news causes confusion regarding the facts of current issues and events (Mitchell, Barthel, Holcomb, & Weisel, 2016). Pew found that this concern is widespread and crosses gender, socioeconomic, age, ethnic, political party, and educational boundaries, with one of the biggest problems being the fact that news consumers do not always recognize fake news when they consume it. 23% of survey respondents stated that they have shared a fake news story, with 14% stating that they knew it was fake when they shared it.

Most librarians will agree with my above assessment that we show our love by sharing news and research. But why do others share it, fake or real? *The New York Times* commissioned a study in 2011 which found that there are five primary motivations for sharing content. Jeff Sonderman of The Poynter Institute breaks them down in this way (Sonderman, 2011):

(1) *Altruism. We share to bring valuable and entertaining content to others. We think about what our friends want to know, and try to help them out.*

(2) *Self-definition. We share to define ourselves to others. Perhaps this notion is better phrased as, "you are what you share." People consciously shape their online persona by the types of things they share.*

(3) *Empathy. We share to strengthen and nourish our relationships. Sharing shows someone else we're thinking about them and we care.*

(4) *Connectedness. We share to get credit and feedback for being a good sharer, to feel valuable in the eyes of others.*

(5) *Evangelism. We share to spread the word about a cause or brand we believe in.*

Interestingly, these five motivations have a commonality in that they are all related to cultivating and nurturing our relationships with others. Apparently, we have more in common with nonlibrarians than we thought!

*The Times* researchers also found that there are six distinct personas that characterize content sharers (Sonderman, 2011):

*(1) Altruists. They are motivated by "empathy, connected-ness, and evangelism." They want to help people out by providing them with content they need.*

*(2) Careerists. They share content in order to build a repu-tation for providing serious content that others find useful.*

*(3) Hipsters. They start conversations and make connections by sharing content.*

*(4) Boomerangs. They want a reaction and to start a debate, regardless of whether or not it is positive or negative.*

*(5) Connectors. They share content in the hopes that it will lead to an offline experience.*

*(6) Selectives. They share specific content with specific individuals, usually through email.*

The motivations and personas identified by *The Times* offer a good explanation of why people share news that they believe to be real. Even when people share fake news that they believe to be true, they are unwitting participants in the spread of fake news.

But what about the sharing of fake news for more nefarious purposes by those who know it is fake? Insight into the motivations of these people can be gleaned by first exploring why people lie. Groundbreaking research by Dr Bella DePaulo, social psychologist at the University of California, Santa Barbara, found that on average, participants in her study, which consisted of 147 adults recording their daily lives and social interactions in a diary, lied once or twice per day (DePaulo, Kashy, Kirkendol, Wyer, & Epstein, 1996). Their reasons for lying included "to try to make themselves look better or feel better, to protect themselves from embarrass-ment or disapproval, or from having their feelings hurt, and to

try to gain the esteem and affection of other people." Lying for
one of these reasons usually results in deception of the "little
white lie" variety – untruths told to spare someone's feelings
(No, really, that dress looks great on you!) or as an excuse
(I'm sorry I'm late but my cat turned off my alarm clock).
However, later research from DePaulo using a similar sample
also revealed that at least one point in each participant's life,
they all told one very serious lie (DePaulo, Ansfield, Kirkendol, & Boden, 2004). DePaulo describes serious lies as
"threats, transgressions, and betrayals that result specifically
in relationship problems, endanger people's reputations, and
are forbidden by organized religion and indictable by law."
Specifically, the most common serious lies involved affairs,
followed by death and serious illnesses, violence, danger,
money, jobs, personal facts and feelings, and identity
(DePaulo et al., 2004). One might wonder why people take
such huge risks in telling serious lies, but DePaulo's premise is
that the truths covered by such lies are even more threatening
than the risks involved in lying (DePaulo et al., 2004).

DePaulo also studied relationship closeness and its effect on
lying. She found that her subjects told their most serious lies
disproportionately by and to their closest relationship partners (DePaulo et al., 2004). It is interesting to note that this
both correlates to and also is unlike sharing content, whether
it is real or fake news. In the content sharing motivation list
reflecting *The New York Times* research, the shares were all
prompted by a desire for connection, in part with those with
whom we already share or desire a strong connection with
(this could be reflected by the altruism, empathy, and
connectedness motivations) or more likely with those with
whom we have weaker connections or with whom we are
trying to establish a connection (the self-definition or evangelism motivations). The same is true of the personas list. The
altruists and selectives are likely to share content with those

with whom they already have strong connections, whereas the careerists, boomerangs, hipsters, and connectors are trying to establish connections.

Whether the connection is strong or weak or is not yet established, the key factor is that again, the share is motivated by relationship. This is not the case when fake news is shared. It is unlikely that those sharing fake news content are carefully considering their audience and the affect that the share will have either on the receiver's perception of the sharer or on the relationship between the receiver and sharer. I did not uncover any research in to this area. I did a search on Google Scholar for "do people consider their relationship with recipients when sharing news via social media" and did not receive any relevant results. I also ran this search in abstracts of academic databases on EbscoHost: (news and (relationship* or connection*) and (share* and (receiv* or recipient* or read))) and received zero results.

When people share fake news that they believe to be true, the first consideration is why they fell for the falsehood in the first place. It isn't because they're dumb; in many cases, it is the attraction of an easy explanation or answer that wins the day. Psychologist Sam Wineburg of the Stanford History Education Group launched a study to try to answer two key questions: why are we so bad at making judgments regarding the veracity of information on the Internet, and how can we get better? (Steinmetz, 2018) He believes that the failure to consider the veracity of search engine results plays a large role, as his team found that trait to be common in Americans of all ages and IQs. Further, research by MIT cognitive scientist David Rand found that people believe fake news 20% of the time, and one possible explanation lies in "fluency heuristics," or a tendency to believe things we've been exposed to in the past. He conducted a study in which subjects were shown headlines in a Facebook-type format. Simply seeing those headlines made people more likely to rate them as factual later on in the experiment; merely viewing something causes the brain to "subconsciously use that as an indication that it's true" (Steinmetz, 2018). But why do people share news, even if they believe it to be true? It is highly likely that one of the above motivations apply.

But what if they are among the 14% of people that knowingly share fake news? Or what if they belong to the population who share without checking to find out whether or not it is fake? The first motivation, and a highly obvious one when outrageous, truly unbelievable content is shared, is that they may be trying to entertain or garner a laugh.

Reinforcing the research findings of Quattrociocchi is Craig Silverman, Media Editor for BuzzFeed. Silverman states that when we read content that reinforces our values and beliefs and confirms what we hold as truth, it makes us feel good. In contrast, when we are confronted with information that goes against our beliefs and values, we don't take pause and analyze what it may mean and whether or not it is true. Instead, we "double down on our existing beliefs" (National Public Radio, 2016). On either side of the coin, whether the content results in anger, hate, surprise, or joy, if the information aligns with our beliefs, it can get us to react. When this situation plays out on social media platforms such as Facebook, it causes us to receive more and more content that is similar to that with which we interact. The danger is that fake news elicits strong emotional reactions and interactions and causes Facebook to add more and more similar content to our newsfeeds (National Public Radio, 2016).

In order to determine how the strong emotional response created by fake news effects the depth and width of its dissemination, researchers at the Massachusetts Institute of Technology (MIT) decided to look into the problem by conducting the largest-ever study to date regarding fake news.

They analyzed 126,000 Twitter cascades – defined as "instances of a rumor spreading pattern that exhibits an unbroken retweet chain with a common, singular origin" – tweeted by over 3 million users during a span of 10 years, and found that "falsehoods are 70% more likely to be retweeted on Twitter than the truth," and "false news reached 1,500 people about six times faster than the truth" (MIT Sloan School of Management, 2018). Additionally, they used two separate metrics to gauge the popularity differential between real and fake news – audience size and network permeation. For example, for a tweet to be retweeted 10,000 times, it could either be tweeted by someone with a million followers and get 10,000 retweets by some of those followers (big but shallow), or someone with few followers could send it out and have it retweeted by one of their followers, who retweets it to their followers, who retweet it to their followers, and so on until it has been retweeted 10,000 times (deep permeation). Either way, fake news dominates. The MIT researchers found that real news was unable to chain together more than 10 retweets, but fake news "could put together a retweet chain 19 links longer and do it 10 times as fast as accurate news put together its measly 10 retweets" (Meyer, 2018).

This begs the question: "Why does falsehood do so well?" The MIT researchers have two theories: fake news is "novel" and different than the other stories in a Twitter user's timeline, and again, those pesky emotions are to blame. As Brendan Nyhan's research has found, "False information online is often really novel and frequently negative. Those are two features of information generally that grab our attention as human beings and that cause us to want to share that information with others" (Meyer, 2018).

The MIT researchers also considered the question of whether or not bots were to blame for the spread of fake news via Twitter. Using two different bot-detection algorithms on a sample of 3 million Twitter users, they found that bots retweeted fake news at the same rate that they retweeted verified news. "The massive difference in how true and false news spreads on Twitter cannot be explained by bots," according to MIT professor Sinan Aral (Meyer, 2018).

When they began the study, the MIT researchers theorized that fake news tweeters would have broad appeal – that they would have more followers than those who tweet accurate news due to the sensational nature of the content they tweet. However, an additional revelation, which *The Atlantic* calls "the most depressing" finding of the study, is that the opposite is true. Fake news tweeters have fewer followers and send fewer tweets than those who share accurate information. Oddly, those who tweet accurate news have been Twitter users for longer than their fake news-tweeting counterparts, and most have verified accounts. "In short, the most trustworthy users can boast every obvious structural advantage that Twitter, either as a company or a community, can bestow on its best users. The truth has a running start, but inaccuracies, somehow, still win the race" (Meyer, 2018).

# 3

# WHEN SHARING IS NOT CARING: FAKE NEWS AND SOCIAL MEDIA

In the 2010 Academy Award-winning film *The Social Network*, Napster founder Sean Parker (played by Justin Timberlake) remarks, "We lived on farms, then we lived in cities, and now we're going to live on the Internet" (IMDb, n.d.). Regardless of whether or not the quote is accurate, it is telling commentary when comparing the Facebook of *The Social Network*, in its nascent stages and the end product of a pursuit-of-the-American-dream-like tale, complete with the Silicon Valley/unicorn startup undertones of whiz kids inventing revolutionary products in a garage, (although this time it was in a Harvard dorm room) with the Facebook of today, which has a valuation of $400 billion and where 44% of Americans get the majority of their news (Tiffany, 2017). Parker could not have envisioned it at the time, but today, "living on the Internet" largely means living on Facebook, "the new front page of the news for over 1 billion people every day" (Shahani, 2016).

In 2003, Harvard sophomore Mark Zuckerberg hacked the school's dormitory ID files and uploaded pictures of his classmates to build a "hot or not" style website called "Facemash." Within days, it was ordered to be taken down by school officials who cited security, copyright, and privacy concerns, but not before over 450 people had voted over 22,000 times regarding which person was "hotter" in a comparison of two ID photos (Weinberger, 2018). Spurred on by his creation's popularity, Zuckerberg launched "Thefacebook" on February 4, 2004. Originally, Thefacebook was for use by Harvard students only and was able to assist students in searching for and finding classmates, identifying friends of friends, and "seeing a visualization of your social network" (Weinberger, 2018). Within a month, half of all Harvard students were members of Thefacebook, and membership was extended to Yale, Stanford, and Columbia, but not before Cameron and Tyler Winklevoss and Divya Narendra raised allegations that Zuckerberg stole their idea after they had tried to hire him to build a similar site, HarvardConnection.com (they reached a settlement agreement with Zuckerberg for $20 million in cash and 1.2 million shares of Facebook stock in 2008) (Carlson, 2010).

By September 2006, Facebook.com offered membership to anyone with an email address, and thus began the journey to becoming the Facebook that we know today, with over 2 billion users sharing everything from photos to videos to news (Statista, 2018). While it is still true that on a basic level, Facebook is a way to connect with others, the current debate stems from whether it is a technology company or a media company, and the responsibilities of each (Kelly, 2018). In August of 2016, Zuckerberg reiterated a familiar position: "We are a tech company, not a media company," (Segreti, 2016) meaning that Facebook has a strictly narrow definition of what that means. Facebook executives have defined media companies as those who create content by employing reporters to do so, whereas by being the conduit and host, they see themselves as a technology company that employs engineers to build the platform that houses the content. This stance lessens the perception of their responsibility for the effects of news on the platform (Griffith, 2017). How one categorizes Facebook's industry, and whether it is technology, media, or a hybrid, plays a large role in one's beliefs regarding the responsibility of Facebook to parse out fake news.

Two days after the 2016 US presidential election, when Zuckerberg was asked if there was a possibility that sensationalized or outright false news stories shared on Facebook helped to fuel the victory of Donald J. Trump, Zuckerberg stated that fake news on Facebook was "a very small amount of the content," and that it was "pretty crazy" to suggest that it had an effect on the outcome (Kokalitcheva, 2016). Immediately, pundits pounced on that statement. Part of Zuckerberg's statement included the fact that "More than 99% of what people see is authentic," but with over a billion users, that remaining 1% can be quite significant (Fiegerman, 2016). Writing in *The New York Times*, associate professor Zeynep Tufekci of the University of North Carolina School of Information and Library Science alleged that Zuckerberg's statement contradicted Facebook's own internal research, citing studies which showed that hundreds of thousands of voters showed up at the polls after seeing a "go vote" message along with photos of their Facebook friends who had clicked on a "I voted" message, and that newsfeeds tweaked with either positive or negative posts prompted readers to respond in kind (Tufekci, 2016). This revelation, coupled with data showing that top 20 fake election stories on Facebook were liked, shared, or commented on over 8.7 million times (Silverman, 2016) prompted Zuckerberg to backpedal less than two weeks later.

## Timeline of Events: Facebook Attempts to Fight Fake News

| Facebook v. Fake News | |
| --- | --- |
| February, 2004 | Mark Zuckerberg launches Thefacebook from his Harvard dorm room |
| September, 2006 | Facebook membership opened to public |
| August, 2016 | Over **1.5 billion** Facebook users |
| November, 2016 | Zuckerberg addresses fake news on Facebook. *"a very small amount of the content;: it is "a pretty crazy idea" to suggest affected the US presidential election* |
| November, 2016 | Facebook rolls out tools to combat the posting of fake news on the platform |
| January, 2017 | Facebook Journalism Project launched |
| January, 2017 | Disputed content flags instituted |
| October, 2017 | "About This Article" system begins |
| December, 2017 | Disputed content tagging system scrapped |
| December, 2017 | Related article linking system unveiled |
| May, 2018 | Facebook posts video, **"Facing Facts,"** detailing their efforts to fight fake news |
| June, 2018 | Info and Ads Tab added |
| July, 2018 | Facebook **changes their focus on fake news** from stopping the posting of fake news to stopping its spread through the newsfeed |
| Sources: Business Insider, Statista, Fortune, CNN, Facebook, The New York Times, newsroom.fb.com | |

In unveiling tools to fight fake news, Zuckerberg stated that Facebook had a responsibility "to take misinformation seriously," yet he reiterated that they did not want to implement editorial controls. "The problems here are complex, both technically and philosophically," he said. "We do not want to be arbiters of truth ourselves, but instead rely on our community and trusted third parties" (Burke, 2016).

The main hallmark of Facebook's fake news safeguards is that they are constantly in flux and being tweaked. One of the first remedies rolled out by Facebook was the ability of users to make stories as false. When this feature was first revealed, it required the user to click on a downward arrow next to the post (later changed to three dots) and click "report post," and then click, "It's a false news story," and then click "Mark this post as false news" (Facebook, 2018). This was later changed to "Give Feedback On This Post," which, when clicked on, prompts the user to choose from a list of categories to label the post: nudity, violence, harassment, suicide or self-injury, false news, spam, unauthorized sales, or hate speech. Only one category can be chosen, even though many posts can be categorized by several labels.

Another remedy is the labeling of articles in the newsfeed with the letter "i." When a user clicks on the I, there is an option on which to click, "Show more information about this article." The user is then shown a description of the source (from Wikipedia), along with a few more selected headlines from that same publication (how these headlines are determined is unclear and they may or may not be related to the article of interest). It also gives a numerical count of how many times the article has been shared, reveals if any of the user's Facebook friends have shared the article, and has a world map with a depiction of share locations (Hughes, Smith, & Leavitt, 2018).

When the article reporting system was in its early stages, Facebook developed a fact-checking network by partnering with media organizations who have committed to a list of ethics issued by The Poynter Institute. When users labeled stories as fake or misleading, Facebook's third-party fact-checkers investigated the claims and labeled and demoted the stories accordingly. Additionally, Facebook crowdsourced this effort by allowing users to tag content which Facebook intended to investigate further. Facebook also has a hate speech algorithm that analyzes content and removes that which it deems offensive, but it has been incorrect on several occasions. When a Pulitzer Prize–winning photo depicting a young girl in the wake of a Vietnam War napalm attack was posted by a Norwegian newspaper, Facebook took it down, citing "display of nudity" (Domonoske, 2016). Facebook also once removed parts of the Declaration of Independence, deeming it to be hate speech (Sandler, 2018a).

Around the same time, Facebook launched the "Facebook Journalism Project," which is "designed to set up 'deeper collaboration' with news organizations, introduce new platforms for telling stories, develop local news, and train journalists and everyday users on finding and trusting news" (Woollaston, 2017). This project prompted the creation of new positions at Facebook, including a "Head of News Partnerships," and others requiring skills in both technology and journalism, signaling an opportunity for all of us in the content business. Despite the constant claims that Facebook did not want to become a media company, fake news somewhat forced its hand. Facebook also disabled the ability of Pages to edit link previews; this editing allowed Pages to "change the headline, body text and image that appeared in the News Feed preview," which was a very easy way to spread fake news (Constine, 2017).

Facebook seemed to be fairly confident in these remedies, yet on December 20, 2017, they issued a blog post in which they announced that "academic research" found that their company-issued "disputed content" flags actually had the opposite effect than that of which they intended; they caused users to become more entrenched in their beliefs and did not preclude sharing of content (Lyons, 2017). As a result, they decided to scrap the system of tagging disputed content, and instead will link posts to "related articles" of factual content and send factual articles to users who share disputed stories (Ghosh, 2017). Additionally, they decided to let users determine news source credibility, by instituting a system of user surveys in which they ask select groups of users whether or not they recognize a publication and how much they trust it. They will then use these survey results to tweak their source ranking algorithm to move posts involving content from sources deemed highly trustworthy to the top of the news feed (Seetharaman, 2018). Facebook also implemented features that provide information about individual pages; specifically, background details on ads. Each Facebook page was given a tab called "Info and Ads"; when a user clicks on the tab, they are given a list of all ads run by that page. This allows users to see not only ads for which they are a target but also all ads running across Facebook (Frenkel, 2018). The "Info and Ads" tab also states when the page was founded and any name changes.

Are these implementations working? Stanford researchers undertook a study to try to find out. They identified 570 false news sites and analyzed social media user interactions with those sites from December 2016 to July 2018 (Allcott, Gentzkow, & Yu, 2018). They found that Facebook user interactions with content from those sites fell 65% during that time period, and that the drop coincided with the institution of the fact-checking program and news feed algorithm tweaks. However, they also found that well after those remedies were instituted, in July, 2018, Facebook users continued to engage with those sites 70 million times (Allcott et al., 2018). "That's a very big number and tells me that Facebook continues to play an important role in the spread of misinformation online," stated Matthew Gentzkow, a Stanford economist who was one of the researchers in the study (Crawford, 2018).

In July of 2018, Facebook came under fire for allowing posts from Holocaust deniers, with Zuckerberg stating that while these posts are "deeply offensive," they will not be taken down, but instead demoted in the newsfeed (Sandler, 2018b). He then clarified Facebook's mission with regard to fake news: their goal is not to prevent the posting of misinformation and fake news, but to stop its spread. Unfortunately, trying to stop the spread of fake news by demoting it in the newsfeed only works when users rely on Facebook's algorithm to curate their newsfeed. This is done by choosing "top stories" as the preference in newsfeed settings. If users choose "most recent," as their setting, and a fake news post from one of their friends or a page that they follow is posted around the time that they open their newsfeed, it will appear. Also, if someone has set a Facebook friend or followed page as "see first," they are going to see it first even if it is fake news.

In the 2018 US midterm elections, Facebook fared better. Non–Facebook affiliated reporters and fact-checkers vigilantly monitored the platform and reported falsehoods and hoaxes to Facebook staff, who worked 24/7 to remove the content (Roose, 2018). While this system allowed Facebook to keep Kremlin-linked troll interference to a minimum, it is unsettling that Facebook is relying on outsiders to find and report fake news, according to Jennifer Grygiel, of Syracuse University, who stated, "It's a bad sign that the war rooms, especially Facebook's war room, didn't have this information first" (Roose, 2018). It is also very uncertain whether or not such a hypervigilant system is sustainable. Jonathan Albright, research director at the Tow Center for Digital Journalism at Columbia University, believes that while Facebook has become better at removing some of the most egregious content, "For blatantly false news, they're not even close to getting ahead of it," he stated. "They're barely keeping up" (Roose, 2018). Also, this type of effort is much more easily undertaken in the United States, since a majority of staff and content monitors are English-speaking Americans and there is cooperation from law enforcement. Facebook has users all over the world; is Facebook responsible for maintaining free and fair elections in those places? Such an undertaking really does seem impossible. As Kevin Roose wrote in *The New York Times*, "If you think Facebook will spin up a 24/7 'war room' to help stop meddling in Nigeria's February elections, I have a bridge in Lagos to sell you" (Roose, 2018).

The main problem with Facebook's solutions is that these efforts fall short when fake news goes viral. By the time that

Facebook's fake news fact-checkers complete their investigations, with each fact-check being completed by a minimum of two Facebook employees, erroneous content and data can take on a life of its own. Also, what is the skillset and academic background of the users whose opinions are being used to determine the trustworthiness of sources? How is their objectivity measured? Whether or not we trust something is largely a matter of opinion; trustworthy does not mean accurate or factual. In response to this sentiment, Zuckerberg wrote, "The hard question we've struggled with is how to decide what news sources are broadly trusted in a world with so much division. We could try to make that decision ourselves, but that's not something we're comfortable with. We considered asking outside experts, which would take the decision out of our hands but would likely not solve the objectivity problem. Or we could ask you – the community – and have your feedback determine the ranking. We decided that having the community determine which sources are broadly trusted would be most objective" (Terdiman, 2018). Unfortunately, he did not consider that librarians take an oath of objectivity and are well qualified to make these determinations. They are part and parcel to our mission, and evaluation of source credibility is one of the most important components of the library school curriculum. We are a natural fit for this role, yet it is unclear whether or not any librarians are being hired to assist Facebook in these efforts.

It seems as though every discussion of Facebook centers around two issues, "Is Facebook a media company?" and "How can Facebook be improved?" The answers to both questions depend largely upon whom you ask. Daphne Keller of the Stanford Center for Internet and Society believes that Section 230 of the Communications Decency Act allows for Facebook to police bad actors on the service and make decisions regarding which content is made available without being liable for users' posts, and this is exactly what Facebook has argued in court when they have faced lawsuits regarding their ability to restrict data access to app developers with objectionable content (Levin, 2018). Santa Clara University law professor Eric Goldman concurs, stating that Facebook "should have the power to stop apps," while Harvard law school professor Rebecca Tushnet believes that in doing so, Facebook is "owning up to the reality that we all see, that it has an important place in the media environment." For Kathleen Culver, journalism professor at the University of Wisconsin, Madison, it is a question of semantics, as she believes that Facebook has a media role that is not easily described by the term "publisher," stating that "the language we have to date does not match the technology that has now been developed" (Levin, 2018).

In October 2017, *The New York Times* contacted tech industry experts and thought leaders and asked them to weigh in on the question, "How Can Facebook Be Fixed?" *The Times* asked the respondents to address not only Facebook's issues regarding allegations of collusion with Russia during the US presidential election, but also its effect on the media industry as a whole and its role in the creation of echo chambers and feedback loops that tell us what we want to hear and keep us coming back for more (Manjoo & Roose, 2017).

Fake accounts plague Facebook, according to Scott Dickens, Facebook product manager (Nicas, 2018). Although they were able to identify and remove around 583 million fake accounts in the first three months of 2018, an April 2018 earnings document revealed that Facebook estimated that 80 million accounts, or roughly 4% of the total, are still fraudulent. In order to close them down, Facebook has to try to outsmart a constant flood of impersonations and fabricated accounts created by increasingly sophisticated techniques. "It's the arms race," Dickens said (Nicas, 2018). Kevin Kelly, cofounder of *Wired* magazine, believes that verifying all accounts to ensure that they belong to real people would go a long way toward fixing the platform, but he doesn't offer specifics regarding how this would work. Past suggestions to verify accounts, such as requiring social security numbers and credit card numbers, could preclude marginalized populations from participating, causing the filter bubble to become even more homogenized. Kelly also believes that offering a filter so that only posts or shares from verified accounts enter a user's newsfeed should be offered, but again, it is unclear how to verify accounts.

Jonathan Albright believes that reactions should be deprioritized in the news feed algorithm, and that reaction buttons for "trust" and "respect" should be added.

Congressman Ro Khanna, who represents California's 17th district, which contains Silicon Valley, in the US House of Representatives, believes that transparency is the key to creating a user population with more trust in Facebook. He wants answers to these questions:

- How does the news feed algorithm work?
- How are data used in creation and distribution of ads?

Vivian Schiller, formerly of NPR, NBC News, and Twitter, in a twist on Donald Rumsfeld's "known unknowns," says Facebook must "come clean" and answer these additional pointed questions:

- What does Facebook know and what do they know that they cannot share?
- What do they not know?
- What do they not know that they don't know?

Finally, Columbia University Law School professor Tim Wu has perhaps the most radical suggestion: that Facebook become a nonprofit. Wu believes that if Facebook did not have to focus on "catering to filter bubbles, addicting and manipulating users, seizing data, bending over backward for advertisers, and destroying competitors," it would be free to focus on Zuckerberg's goals for the platform, which include "bringing us closer together," and "building a global community" (Manjoo & Roose, 2017).

By April 2015, Twitter was in trouble. Both the number of account holders actively tweeting and creation of new accounts were in decline, (Edwards, 2015) and by June of 2016, TheStreet ran an article with the headline, "Election 2016 Will Make or Break Twitter," stating that the presidential contest might represent Twitter's last chance to prove "its still relevant and knows how to make money" (Stewart, 2016). Enter "The Trump Effect." According to analysis by *Fortune*, Trump's use of Twitter, coinciding with his announcement of his candidacy and increasing primary wins, had a direct correlation with spikes in the number of active users as well as increases in profit, revenue, and stock price (Morris, 2018). Considering the fact that Trump tweets, on average, 6–7 times per day, and that his tweets "set the tone for a national conversation on a daily basis," it is almost impossible to keep abreast of breaking news without using Twitter (Estepa, 2017).

A groundbreaking study of the diffusion of over 126,000 true and false new stories distributed via Twitter from 2006 to 2017 found that fake news outperforms the truth in three distinct ways: it reaches people faster, it penetrates networks deeper, and it spreads faster. At first glance, it seems logical that perhaps bots played a role, but according to MIT data scientist Soroush Vosoughi, the lead researcher of the study, "it might have something to do with human nature"

(Meyer, 2018). First, the MIT team that conducted the study believe that fake news is "more novel" than real news. They used a system of novelty metrics to calculate the information distance between rumor tweets and all prior tweets that users were exposed to before retweeting the rumor tweets and found that false rumors were perceived as more novel than truth across all applied novelty metrics (Vosoughi, Roy, & Aral, 2018). Second, they believe that fake news elicits stronger emotional responses than truth, prompting shares. In order to test that theory, they assessed users' perceptions of the information in the tweets by comparing emotional content of true and false rumors. They found that false rumors initiated more "surprise" and "disgust" feeling replies, whereas true news initiated more sadness, anticipation, and trust replies, so it is possible that the falsehood emotions prompted more tweets and retweets of fake news. Regarding bots, the found that "the greater likelihood of people to retweet falsity more than the truth is what drives the spread of false news," and that "human behavior contributes more to the differential spread of falsity and truth than automated robots do" (Vosoughi et al., 2018). Their ultimate conclusion was that "false news is more novel and that novel information is more likely to be retweeted," and that "false information online is often really novel and frequently negative" (Vosoughi et al., 2018, p. 45).

Testifying before British lawmakers in February 2018, Nick Pickles, Twitter's head of public policy for the United Kingdom, stated, "We are not the arbiters of truth. We are not going to remove content based on the fact that this is untrue" (Borchers, 2018). Twitter spokeswoman Emily Horne held this party line in June 2017, stating that Twitter had "no current plans to launch" a rumored system to allow users to flag tweets as fake news (Dwoskin, 2017). However, by the summer of 2018, Twitter began to institute safeguards to try to identify dubious users. In order to police fraudulent accounts, Twitter began requiring an email address or phone number in order to sign up for the service; this will be double-checked through a "security check" instituted by Twitter to try to prevent automated sign-ups, which Twitter stated has stopped more than 50,000 fake account openings per day (Wang, 2018).

Twitter also began analyzing individual tweets by studying "behavioral signals," such as users who tweet at a large amount of accounts that they don't follow, users who follow accounts tagged as spam or bots, how often users block each other, and instances of many accounts being created from a single IP address. Twitter then either suspends the accounts or places them lower in the message stream (Timberg & Dwoskin, 2018). They are also placing warning signals on suspicious accounts and not allowing new users to follow them (Timberg & Dwoskin, 2018, p. 51). Regarding their ad system, Twitter introduced an "Ads Transparency Center," which is basically a database of all ads run on the platform, albeit one that does not allow for keyword searches. That limitation makes it impossible to search for ads run on specific topics such as gun control or immigration; users can only see advertisements distributed for specific buyers (Frenkel, 2018).

Even though fake news funneled through Google has been estimated to be less than 3% (Kan, 2018), with a mobile search market share of over 93%, Google is the dominant delivery mechanism of information searched for on the Internet and a major player in news in general (Statista, 2018). In response to allegations of fake news and erroneous information appearing in search result lists, Google first developed Fact Check, which is a labeling system which utilizes an algorithm to look for news articles that "fact check" certain statements and declarations. When the algorithm locates a fact-checking article, that article is linked to the corresponding

search result (Kosslyn & Yu, 2017). However, if several
fact-checking articles contradict themselves, the algorithm
does not determine which one is correct. Therefore, search
results could have fact checks of conflicting information.
There is also the possibility that the fact-checked article is
wrong, or that an article written to deliberately mislead will be
tagged. Google also announced that they no longer depriori-
tize articles behind paywalls in the list of search results (Stein,
2017). While this is a small, albeit admirable step toward
ensuring that credible news is listed, many were taken aback
at this announcement, having not been aware that this was a
Google procedure. In July of 2018, Google announced a set of
news initiatives that use "the best of artificial intelligence to
find the best of human intelligence," according to the product
chief, Trystan Upstill (Calhoun, 2018). Basically, Google has
written programming algorithms to (Gingras, 2018):

- Emphasize authoritative results over freshness or relevancy
  during a period of breaking news or in crisis situations;
- Highlight verified news content in a "Breaking News"
  section on YouTube and a "Top News" shelf in search
  results;
- Power the Google News app to provide content in six
  distinct areas: briefing (five stories chosen based off of user
  history and location), full coverage (deep dive stories from
  trustworthy sources), favorites (signals Google to source
  from the user's favorite news sites), less, please (allows the
  user to request fewer stories on a topic), save stories (allows
  the user to read stories later), and get subscriptions (allows
  the user to manage subscriptions in the news app and also
  subscribe using a Google account) (Calhoun, 2018).

Whereas *The New York Times* asked experts for remedies
specifically for Facebook flaws, *The Economist* issued a

briefing in November 2017 that took a look at strategies that could be applied to social media platforms in general (*The Economist*, 2017a). Harvard University fellow Wael Ghonim suggests that social media platforms provide a detailed view of information distribution, complete with data on how far the content has spread and who has seen it. This call for transparency would also require labeling of bots and fake accounts. Another suggestion from *The Economist*, issued before the MIT research that found that people like to share fake news even when told it is fake, is to have pop-up warnings appear when users click on articles that state, "Do you really want to share this? This news item has been found to be false." Also issued before the MIT research was released but completely in-line with the findings regarding emotional response, is the suggestion to "redirect" users to "calmer content," after they react to or share stories with negative or hostile themes (*The Economist*, 2017a).

*The Economist* also discussed the issuance of monetary fines for social media companies who do not remove hate speech expediently. For example, Germany has the distinction of being among the first countries to regulate false and incendiary posts on social media, requiring that companies take down hate speech and fake news within 24 hours or face steep fines (*The Economist*, 2017a). Inspired by the German example, a UK parliamentary committee recommended that a "stronger law" and "system of fines" be considered for companies that do not remove hate speech on their networks (Burgess, 2017). On multiple occasions, judges in Brazil have blocked access to WhatsApp on similar grounds. Finally, if there is a reluctance for government intervention, it might be possible for those who can prove they were "directly and concretely harmed by the spread of fake news" to sue for defamation (Lazer et al., 2018). Since in the United States, the 1996 Communications Decency Act offers "near-comprehensive immunity" to the hosting platforms regarding content created by others, any changes to this legal regime would raise "thorny issues about the extent to which platform content and content-curation decisions should be subject to second-guessing" (Lazer et al., 2018). In the European Union, however, the "right to be forgotten," and General Data Protection Regulation (GDPR) are providing for removal of personal data and content from search engine results, and this could have broader implications that eventually extend to social media (Tiku, 2018).

# 4

# HOW TO SPOT FAKE NEWS

Pierre Salinger spent a lifetime as an eyewitness to history, first as a press secretary to John F. Kennedy, and later, as an ABC News correspondent (Lueck, 2004). He was a well-known, esteemed, highly credible journalist whose integrity and intelligence were without question, so many were taken aback when, in 1997, he fell for an Internet hoax that stated that a TWA flight was accidentally shot down by a United States Navy missile. After viewing fake documents on the Internet, Salinger became convinced that this was true; he contacted the FBI and then-US Defense Secretary William Cohen and held a press conference to reveal his findings (Reid, 2006). At the time, the strange episode was dismissed as a sad ending to a storied career, but not before the concept of falling for Internet conspiracy theories became known as "Pierre Salinger syndrome."

Fast-forward to the fake news era, and "Pierre Salinger syndrome" seems downright quaint. Who would have ever guessed that we would now be living in an era where fake news travels faster than the truth? Looking backward, it is hard to believe that there was actually a time when a press conference was called to reveal sensational Internet findings. By 2018, there weren't enough podiums and microphones in the world to handle all of the press conferences that would have to be held if we did so every time someone fell for fake news.

This chapter contains tools and resources for librarians to use in applying and teaching information literacy skills. Perhaps I am a bit jaded, but before one even begins the evaluation process, I recommend starting from a place of assuming that everything is possibly fake news, and go from there. In a twist on "guilty until proven innocent," information evaluation is a process where it is prudent to assume the worst. Then, if the research in question passes the trust tests in the spotting guides discussed in this chapter, a determination that the information is credible can be made.

It is also wise, when consuming news and information, to hit the pause button. Claire Wardle, director of First Draft, a nonprofit dedicated to improving trust in journalism, says, "In the same way that you're told to wait 20 minutes before you reach for a second helping of food because you need to wait for your brain to catch up with your stomach, the same is true with information. Maybe you don't need to wait 20 minutes before clicking the share button, but two minutes is probably sensible" (Wardle, 2017).

When we think of the type of content that constitutes fake news, we often think of it as popular press. However, academic research is not immune. Authors Helen Pluckrose, James A. Lindsay and Peter Boghossian undertook a project in which they spent a year writing 20 articles using fabricated research. Of the 20, four were successfully published and three were accepted for later publication, along with seven under review and six rejected. While the academic legitimacy of the majority of the journals to which the papers were submitted is tenuous, a few did have significant standing, prompting Harvard University political scientist Yascha Mounk to remark, "What they have shown is that certain journals, and perhaps to an extent certain fields, can't distinguish between serious scholarship and a ridiculous intellectual hoax" (Shuessler, 2018).

How can librarians and information professionals evaluate the contents of academic journals, since they are likely to be outside of our field? Harvard Business Review recommends that researchers never rely on only one study to draw conclusions. "Whenever possible, look for meta-analyses or systematic reviews that synthesize results from many studies, as they can provide more-credible evidence and sometimes suggest reasons why results differ," cautions Eva Vivalt of Australian National University (Vivalt, 2018). Further, consider the sample size of the tested population; studies using a small sample are very difficult to replicate. Finally, it is important to understand how the population sample was chosen. Ask yourself: "How did the researchers come to study the people, firms, or products they did? Would you expect this sample to have performed better or worse than the sample you are interested in? Was there anything special about the setting that could have made the results larger?" (Vivalt, 2018).

Academic librarians in universities have long taught information literacy workshops and classes to undergraduates and other staff, and usually, at one point during the instruction, a checklist of criteria to use in evaluating information integrity for use in academic research papers is distributed. Sarah Blakeslee of California State University, Chico, had taught her share of these courses, but in the Spring of 2004, she found herself wondering if there might be an easier way to remember the items on the checklist. Could she develop an acronym or mnemonic to help students remember the steps they should take when evaluating information? It was out of this question that the CRAAP test was born, and because of Blakeslee's work, "for every source of information, we would now have a handy frame of reference to inquire, 'Is this CRAAP?'" (Blakeslee, 2004).

## The CRAAP Test

### Evaluating Information – Applying the CRAAP Test
Meriam Library 📖 California State University, Chico

When you search for information, you're going to find lots of it . . . but is it good information? You will have to determine that for yourself, and the **CRAAP Test** can help. The **CRAAP Test** is a list of questions to help you evaluate the information you find. Different criteria will be more or less important depending on your situation or need.

Key: ■ indicates criteria is for Web

### Evaluation Criteria

**C**urrency: *The timeliness of the information.*
- When was the information published or posted?
- Has the information been revised or updated?
- Does your topic require current information, or will older sources work as well?
- ■Are the links functional?

**R**elevance: *The importance of the information for your needs.*
- Does the information relate to your topic or answer your question?
- Who is the intended audience?
- Is the information at an appropriate level (i.e. not too elementary or advanced for your needs)?
- Have you looked at a variety of sources before determining this is one you will use?
  Would you be comfortable citing this source in your research paper?

**A**uthority: *The source of the information.*
- Who is the author/publisher/source/sponsor?
- What are the author's credentials or organizational affiliations?
- Is the author qualified to write on the topic?
- Is there contact information, such as a publisher or email address?
- ■Does the URL reveal anything about the author or source?
  examples: .com .edu .gov .org .net

**A**ccuracy: *The reliability, truthfulness and correctness of the content.*
- Where does the information come from?
- Is the information supported by evidence?
- Has the information been reviewed or refereed?
- Can you verify any of the information in another source or from personal knowledge?
- Does the language or tone seem unbiased and free of emotion?
- Are there spelling, grammar or typographical errors?

**P**urpose: *The reason the information exists.*
- What is the purpose of the information? Is it to inform, teach, sell, entertain or persuade?
- Do the authors/sponsors make their intentions or purpose clear?
- Is the information fact, opinion or propaganda?
- Does the point of view appear objective and impartial?
- Are there political, ideological, cultural, religious, institutional or personal biases?

9/17/10

The first component of the CRAAP evaluation criteria is currency, or the timeliness of the information. This can be evaluated by considering the publication date, whether or not it has been updated, and if the time period in which the document was created is still applicable to the research project.

The second CRAAP component is relevance, or whether or not the information is related to the project. Additional questions regarding relevance include consideration of the intended audience and the educational level for which the information is written, as well as evaluation of the research in comparison with other sources on the same topic. CRAAP cautions the user to consider if they would be "comfortable citing this source in your research paper" (Blakeslee, 2004).

Authority, or the source of the information, is the third component of the CRAAP test. The authority test requires consideration of the author and their credentials, and whether or not they are qualified to write about the topic at hand. It also involves analysis of the author or publisher's contact information, and what its URL reveals about the source. For example, URLs with a .edu, .gov, or .org address might indicate a nonprofit, which is sometimes seen as more objective than a corporate source. The Gumberg Library of Duquesne University takes the authority component a step further with the reminder that authority is contextual, and that the author's education and expertise needs to be related to the subject matter. "Having a PhD in Astronomy would not give someone authority to write about the impact of music therapy on children who have autism. The expertise or experience needs to be relevant to the topic" (Gumberg Library, 2018).

Component four, accuracy, underlies the other components and is the most important because it involves analysis of the "reliability, truthfulness, and correctness of the content," which is the ultimate goal in information literacy (Wardle, 2017). In determining accuracy, the source of the information and substantiating evidence need to be considered. The CRAAP test also asks if the information is from a peer-reviewed or refereed journal, if it has been discussed in other sources, if the language and tone is appropriate, and also, if it contains grammatical or spelling errors.

The fifth component asks the question of why the information exists. What is its purpose? Is it to "inform, teach, sell, entertain, or persuade?" (Wardle, 2017). Do the authors make their intentions clear in a way that is objective and impartial? Are there any biases? Is it fact, an opinion piece, or propaganda?

When Oxford Dictionaries chose "post-truth" as their Word of the Year for 2016, the International Federation of

---

**IFLA's Guide to Spotting Fake News**

# HOW TO SPT FAKE NEWS

### CONSIDER THE SOURCE
Click away from the story to investigate the site, its mission and its contact info.

### READ BEYOND
Headlines can be outrageous in an effort to get clicks. What's the whole story?

### CHECK THE AUTHOR
Do a quick search on the author. Are they credible? Are they real?

### SUPPORTING SOURCES?
Click on those links. Determine if the info given actually supports the story.

### CHECK THE DATE
Reposting old news stories doesn't mean they're relevant to current events.

### IS IT A JOKE?
If it is too outlandish, it might be satire. Research the site and author to be sure.

### CHECK YOUR BIASES
Consider if your own beliefs could affect your judgement.

### ASK THE EXPERTS
Ask a librarian, or consult a fact-checking site.

IFLA
International Federation of Library Associations and Institutions

Library Associations and Institutions (IFLA) seized the opportunity to position librarians and information professionals as the go-to resource for training and education in critical thinking skills regarding media literacy. Using Factcheck.org's "How To Spot Fake News" article as a framework, IFLA built an infographic to serve as a guide and checklist for determining information veracity; it has since been translated into 36 different languages (IFLA, 2017).

Step one in the IFLA infographic is "Consider The Source." This can be done by reading the "about us" section of a website to determine the mission of a website, its owners and operators, and its contact information. Domain names should also be considered. For example, websites ending in "lo" such as Newslo often mix accurate and inaccurate information. Similarly, sites that end in .com.co or .news, such as msnbc.news, are often fake versions of real news sites. Domain names ending in .ru can be dubious, and those ending in .wordpress are typically personal blogs (Zimdars, 2016a). That is not to say that they are sources of fake news, but blogs do not undergo the same editorial process as those from traditional news sources.

IFLA's second step is "Check the Author." This includes determining if the author is "real," and also, considering the meaning of articles that do not have an author listed. If no one is standing behind the information presented, that could be a red flag. Also, if the author is a blogger, the above caveat applies; their work did not undergo a rigorous editorial process by a third party.

Marydee Ojala, editor in chief of *Online Searcher* magazine, offers an admonishment that might not immediately come to mind when applying IFLA's third step of checking the date of the article. "There's one date that is a dead giveaway that this is fake news – April 1. Never confuse an April Fool's prank with real news" (Ojala, 2017). In checking the date, it is also important to consider your audience and the purpose of your research. Older articles that might be completely on point for one particular research project may not be useful when sending out news alerts or updates on certain companies, industries, or subject matter.

IFLA's admonishment to "check your biases" is fairly straightforward; every interaction and experience that we have as individuals helps to shape our worldview and can affect the way that we interpret what we read. However, these same values and beliefs make it difficult to objectively determine if we are biased. When her students started citing dubious sources in research papers along with referring to them as authoritative outlets in classroom discussions, Dr Melissa Zimdars, assistant professor of communication at Merrimack College, decided to compile a list of "Misleading, Clickbait-y, and Satirical 'News' Sources" as a guide (Zimdars, 2016b). The result is OpenSources (www.opensources.co), a continuously updated database of information sources, each of which undergoes a six-part analysis process and then is tagged with a news-type classification label. The analysis process takes into consideration factors such as domain name, information in the "about us" section, source veracity, and whether or not the source follows a respected style guide such as AP. Zimdars and her team also undertake two lesser-known source analysis procedures. They evaluate the overall esthetics of the website, taking into account whether or not it is cluttered or photoshopped, and they apply a social media metric, looking for clickbait and articles whose content do not reflect their headlines. After the sources are analyzed, they are tagged with one of the following labels (Zimdars, 2016b):

(1)  Fake News

   • Content is fabricated, deceptive, or grossly distorted.

(2)  Satire
  • Content uses humor, irony, exaggeration, ridicule, or false information.

(3)  Extreme Bias
  • Content comes from a particular point of view that may rely on propaganda, information that is out of context, and opinions made to look like facts.

(4)  Conspiracy Theory
  • Content from "well-known promoters of kooky conspiracy theories." (Zimdars, 2016b)

(5)  Rumor Mill
  • Content involving rumors, gossip, innuendo, and unverified claims.

(6)  State News
  • Content from countries under government sanction.

(7)  Junk Science
  • Content involving pseudoscience, metaphysics, naturalistic fallacies, and dubious scientific claims.

(8)  Hate News
  • Content involving racism, misogyny, homophobia, and other forms of discrimination.

(9)  Clickbait
  • Content with headlines that do not correlate with the information in the article, even if it is credible.

(10)  Proceed with Caution
  • Content that may be reliable but needs to be verified.

(11)  Political
  • Content reflecting distinct political orientations.

(12)  Credible

- Content generated through practices consistent with traditional, ethical journalism.

Article headlines can cause us to interpret the text before we even read it. For example, if a headline makes us mad, that might be the point. Headlines are also sometimes written in all capital letters to incite outrage or anger by lending the impression of screaming. *Chicago Tribune* reporter Rex Huppke tweeted about exactly that, posting "Prior to the Trump Administration, I never would have been allowed to write a column in all caps" (Huppke, 2018a). Therefore, IFLA's fourth caveat, to "read beyond," means that the user should go beyond the headline to carefully consider the content. This also involves looking for a lack of quotes in the article – if no one stands behind the alleged facts, they might be false.

IFLA's sixth step is to click on the links to any supporting source documents. It is important to determine if the source references are actually applicable to the story itself. Similarly, if only one news outlet is reporting information that seems to be critical or emergent, it is important to look further to make sure it is true.

Perhaps one of the most overused idioms in the English language is "truth is stranger than fiction," and it probably has become even prolific in recent years, as it is becoming harder and harder to separate real news from fake. This is especially true as satire becomes more and more realistic and sophisticated. IFLA suggests that we ask ourselves, "Is it a joke?" when evaluating news. This is easier said than done. While many comedic websites have legal and disclaimer sections that reveal their intention, when credible news websites also feature satirical writing, it can become extremely confusing. For example, at first glance, "The Borowitz Report," which is often posted on Facebook, seems to be a real *New Yorker* news post (Borowitz,

2017a). One of particular note featured a Getty image of Trump press secretary Sean Spicer at the White House podium, with the headline, "Disturbed Man Gets Past White House Security, Gives Press Conference." Another stated, "Americans Overwhelmingly Say Lives Have Improved Since Kellyanne Conway Went Away" (Borowitz, 2017b).

These postings are from the real *New Yorker* Facebook account from which *The New Yorker* posts links to their hard news and commentary, and their real website address is listed. However, in the middle of each graphic, it states that this is "Not The News." The fact that this is the only indication that this is a joke underscores how hard it can be to detect humor. Doris Helfer, Chair of Collection Development and Access Services at California State University, Northridge, advises librarians to always add context when sharing satire or humor. For example, if she were sharing a Borowitz *New Yorker* post, Helfer would preface the post with a line such as "I love the satire of the Borowitz Report." In doing so, she gives an immediate "heads up" that the content is not to be taken as truth.

Fake tweets are another major source of fake news. The below fake tweet which went viral in April of 2013 serves as an excellent illustration of the main points to check in determining *real* v. *fake* tweets:

**AP** The Associated Press ⊘
@AP

## Breaking: Two Explosions in the White House and Barack Obama is injured

↰ Reply  ⟳ Retweet  ★ Favorite  ••• More

**1,900**   **83**
RETWEETS   FAVORITES

1:07 PM - 23 Apr 13

Upon examination of the tweet, at first glance, it appears to be tweeted from a real Associated Press Twitter account because it contains the blue check mark that indicates that it is a Twitter-verified account. In this case, the real account was hacked and used, but it is important to note that the check mark can easily be cut and pasted to make a new tweet. Next, the tweeting account has very few followers and no previous tweets. Considering the text of the tweet, first, it has no corroboration. Only the fake Associated Press account associated with this tweet was reporting this information. Second, standard protocols were ignored. A real AP tweet would refer to "President Obama," not "Barack Obama." Finally, the tweet had no attribution; the source of the information was unclear. Real AP tweets on subjects of this nature usually begin with the source of the information (Affelt, 2017).

Tweets sent by automated accounts are another huge concern, and Twitter is recognizing and responding to the problem; in July 2018, they deactivated over two million bot accounts. Spotting bot accounts requires a different set of evaluation criteria; Rex Huppke of *The Chicago Tribune* lists two telltale signs: Twitter handles that consist of words or names followed by a series of random numbers, and "a striking similarity in what the accounts are tweeting" (Huppke, 2018b). For example, during the November 2018 controversy involving CNN's Chief White House correspondent, Jim Acosta, and allegations that he attacked a White House aide who tried to take his microphone, bot accounts were all tweeting either "Acosta assaulted that woman," or "He karate chopped her arm" (Huppke, 2018b). These bot tweets then prompted the creation of a fake video that sped up and zoomed in on Acosta's arms, making them look like they were making a karate chop motion (Huppke, 2018b).

A 2015 project by the Defense Advanced Research Projects Agency (DARPA) resulted in a list of five data points that can be used as a checklist in determining bot accounts (Knight, 2018a):

(1)  User Profile
   - No photo or bio is suspect; if there is a photo, is it generic?

(2)  Syntax
   - Formulaic, repetitive, or "robotic" language along with a lack of understanding of context or changing subjects without segue are red flags.

(3)  Semantics
   - Bot accounts are usually only about one topic or contain the same link posted repeatedly.

(4)  Behavior
   - Tweeting at a very rapid pace, at odd times, or with a viewpoint that is inconsistent over time are hallmarks of bot accounts.

(5)  Followers/Following
   - Bots usually follow few accounts but may be followed by a lot of other bots; often the bot account and its followers are very different with regard to topic and viewpoint, which may mean that they did not manually choose to connect.

Sometimes, certain types of events will precipitate fake news; voting and elections are good examples. When Election Day finally rolls around, the season of fake political news, misleading ads, and dubious mailers should come to a close, but unfortunately, it is exactly when misleading information surrounding the activity of actual voting kicks into high gear.

*The New York Times* featured a list of six common types of
Election Day misinformation and how to avoid them (Roose,
2018):

(1)  Polling Place Hoaxes
  •  False rumors abound regarding activities at polling
     stations. These types of rumors, such as the 2016 claim
     that Immigration and Customs Enforcement (ICE)
     officials were arresting people at the polls, are meant to
     intimidate voters and squelch turnout.

(2)  Remote Voting Options
  •  In 2016, various social media accounts posted that
     voters could cast ballots via text, email, and "over
     the Internet." Only certain overseas absentee voters
     who qualify under the Uniformed and Overseas
     Citizens Absentee Voting Act can submit ballots
     over the Internet, and no state offers voting by
     texting.

(3)  Suspicious Texts
  •  Texts stating that "voting hours or locations have
     changed, that new forms of voter ID are required, or
     that your voter registration is not valid" (Roose, 2018)
     are probably fake.

(4)  Voting Machine Malfunction Rumors
  •  "Reports of broken, rigged or technically compro-
     mised voting machines are common on Election Day,"
     along with "videos of malfunctioning voting machines
     going viral on social media" (Roose, 2018). The best
     response to these reports is to triple check your
     choices when voting electronically and notify poll
     workers if there seems to be a problem with your
     voting machine.

(5)   Misleading Photos and Videos
- We've all seen myriad video footage and photos of ridiculously long lines at the polls. Remember that they could be altered or falsely captioned.

(6)   False Voter Fraud Allegations
- Voter fraud is extremely rare. According to the Brennan Center for Justice, an American has a better chance of being struck by lightning than to be found impersonating another voter at the polls (Brennan Center for Justice, 2017). Further, a 2014 Harvard study found that "the likely percent of non-citizen voters in recent US elections is 0" (Brennan Center for Justice, 2017).

*The New York Times* also issued a list of action steps to be undertaken in order to avoid misinformation surrounding elections (Roose, 2018):

- Rely on official government websites or independent, nonpartisan organizations such as Vote411 and Ballot-Ready for voting and election information.
- Use fact-checking websites and reverse image searches to see if information is false, outdated, mislabeled, or altered.
- Report voter intimidation to poll workers, the Election Protection Hotline of the Lawyers' Committee for Civil Rights Under Law at 1-866-OUR-VOTE, or the Department of Justice Voting Rights Hotline at 1-800-253-3931.
- Use social media fake news reporting tools to label and report misinformation.

BrightLocal's 2017 Local Customer Review Survey found that while 85% of consumers trust reviews as much as recommendations from friends, 79% have read a fake review within the past year (BrightLocal, 2017). Two websites dedicated to rooting out fake reviews are Fakespot.com and Reviewmeta.com. Fakespot.com's algorithm automatically analyzes reviews when users enter links to product pages. The algorithm looks for suspicious reviews by considering poor grammar and spelling, overuse of words like "great" and "amazing," and the number of reviews written by each reviewer, along with their purchasing patterns. It also looks for mismatched dates. Fakespot then assigns the product a letter grade based upon the number of reviews and the percentage deemed unreliable. On Reviewmeta.com, when a user pastes in a product link, the algorithm either strips out or reduces the weight of certain reviews, leaving the user with an adjusted rating. Interestingly, the elimination of reviews as unreliable does not always indicate that the overall score is falsely inflated. In an example using reviews of a set of headphones, over 400 Amazon reviewers gave the product an average of 4.7 stars. Even though Reviewmeta's algorithm eliminated over 200 reviews as unreliable, the headphones still garnered an average rating of 4.4 stars (Broida, 2017).

Spotting fake health-related news requires a slightly different checklist; sometimes it can literally be a matter of life and death! As a BBC article stated, "If news stories about politics can influence voting patterns, then could health stories about unproven treatments result in people eschewing their current medical treatment in favor of the latest recommendation in an article they see?" (Hammond, 2017) Consider the plight of expectant parents who are looking for more information regarding the vitamin K shots administered to all newborns in the first few hours of life. Infants are born with less vitamin K than is required, and these shots help to prevent potential bleeding, but a Google search for "vitamin K shot" results in hits such as "Skip that Newborn

Vitamin K Shot." The CDC website does not appear until the 4th result (DiResta, 2018). Michael Golebiewski of Bing refers to this as a "data void"; that is, when a search for answers using a keyword results in "content produced by a niche group with a particular agenda" (DiResta, 2018). In the case of vitamin K, these results are not unique to Google; searches for the keyword on Facebook result in anti-vaccination articles, and searches for it on YouTube return videos of noted conspiracy theorist Alex Jones in the top 10 results (DiResta, 2018).

Two *Atlantic* writers, Nat Gyenes and An Xiao Mina, coined the term "misinfodemics" to describe "the spread of a particular health outcome or disease facilitated by viral misinformation" (Gyenes & Mina, 2018). The "anti-vax" movement aptly illustrates this phenomenon. In 2000, the Centers for Disease Control (CDC) declared that measles had been eradicated in the United States. Fast forward to 2018, and measles outbreaks were reported in Portland, Boston, Chicago, and Michigan. Researchers attribute these out-breaks to a lack of immunization due to fear of vaccines, which is directly linked to misleading content on the Internet (Gyenes & Mina, 2018). According to Gyenes and Mina, a single article linking the measles vaccine to autism is responsible for almost all cases of measles vaccine reluctance (Gyenes & Mina, 2018). Although the author's medical license was revoked and the article retracted after revelations of "serious financial conflicts of interest," (the author was in the process of filing a patent for an alternative measles vaccine), "unethical data collection," (the author paid guests at his son's 10th birthday party to provide blood samples), and fraud, the damage was done once the article's precepts became known.

The tenets of the article were reported on "CNN iReport," a CNN website that allows anyone to upload stories that are "not edited, fact-checked, or screened before they post" (CNN, n.d.). By October of 2014, the article and a follow-up to it, also on the CNN iReport, had "more than 786,000 views and 256,000 shares on social media," and viral YouTube videos about Hooker's hypotheses had over 124,000 views" (Lupkin, 2014). Further confirmation of the viral nature of anti-vax material comes from researchers from Virginia Commonwealth University, who found that 75% of Pinterest posts related to vaccines discuss the false link between measles vaccines and autism (Guidry, Carlyle, Messner, & Jin, 2015), and a study from George Washington University which found that bot accounts on Twitter tweeted about vaccines 22 more times than real Twitter users (Glenza, 2018).

Sadly, the article, "Fraud at the CDC Uncovered, 340% Risk of Autism Hidden From Public," remains posted on the site as of September 6, 2018, along with a caveat paragraph at the top from CNN that states "This story, which is about a study from Dr Brian Hooker about the alleged link between vaccines and autism, was initially pulled for further review after it was flagged by the community. CNN has reached out to the CDC for comment and is working to confirm the claims in this iReport" (eplettner, 2014). The bottom line is that CNN is a trusted source of news to the general public, and it is unclear how many readers of the CNN iReport understand that its contents are not actually from CNN. Perhaps even more sadly, if readers had taken the basic step in both the CRAPP and IFLA documents, to "consider the source," (granted, they would have needed to recognize that they were not looking at an actual CNN article, which makes source review much more difficult), it is highly likely that at least some cases of measles and possibly even subsequent deaths could have been avoided.

Creators of fake health news often combine bits and pieces of hard scientific evidence and slice and dice them to capitalize on the public's hopes of medical breakthroughs and miracle cures. Tim Caulfield, Director of the Health Law Institute at the University of Alberta, calls this "science-ploitation"; that is, when someone leverages real science and its surrounding excitement and uses it to "push nonsense" (CBC Radio, 2018b). Caulfield and his colleagues studied stem cell research and its portrayal on fake news websites. They found that fake health news websites "rely on conspiracy theories and promote fear and mistrust of conventional medicine," and are usually in the business of either prompting clicks in order to sell ads, or they are aligned with companies that sell products or own clinics offering unregulated stem cell treatments (CBC Radio, 2018b). This is particularly dangerous, according to Caulfield, because it causes fake news to become the driver of this industry, generating millions of dollars in revenue for companies offering treatments that have resulted in medical malpractice and even death (CBC Radio, 2018b).

Unfortunately, sometimes even doctors themselves inadvertently contribute to the spread of fake health news, as passing comments and singular studies become blown out of proportion and touted as miracle cures. Dr Caroline Hamm, an oncologist and clinical director of the Windsor Cancer Research Group in Windsor, Ontario, decided to study dandelion root tea after three of her patients reported higher white blood cell counts after drinking it. She mentioned this to one patient, and soon, a plethora of stories about dandelion root as a cure for cancer began cropping up on the Internet. Dr Hamm began to receive emails from all over the world with inquiries from cancer patients who want to stop standardized cancer treatment and drink dandelion root tea instead. Now she devotes much of her time to snuffing out these false claims. "It's a lot of work that takes us away from our patient care. It's also very hard to talk to these people. Someone's offered them false hope and you have to take it away from them," she stated. In retrospect, she wishes that she would have tried to "stay out of the news," to begin with (CBC Radio, 2018a).

According to Renee DiResta, of the Berkman Klein Center of Harvard University, the reason for lack of factual counter-content is relatively simple: no one feels the need to produce it, and even if they did, it is unlikely to go viral. Further, when a plethora of fake news stories result when searching on a keyword, it isn't because the message represents the conventional wisdom, but rather is a result of these niche groups having thousands of members who thrive on social media and oftentimes pay for ad campaigns to reinforce their beliefs (DiResta, 2018).

It is always important to investigate the journal in which research is being reported, but in judging the veracity of medical news, peer review is critical. Peer-reviewed journals only contain articles that are read, scrutinized, and reviewed by other scientists working in the same field prior to being published. Also, the plausibility of the claim needs to be considered. The more groundbreaking the development, the more evidence needed to confirm its validity. Massive break-throughs "will have been tested on thousands of patients, published in medical journals, and covered by the biggest media around the world." If it is a drug-related "miracle cure," it is important to verify that the drug has entered the human trial phase. Many promising drugs are reported on, but until they reach human trials, they have a long way to go before they will be available for purchase by patients (Affelt, 2017).

Some articles use the provocative headline of, "The Secret That Even Doctors Won't Tell You," in order to get a high count of people clicking on them. They then use these numbers to sell ads. It is unlikely that doctors know of effective treatments but are keeping them from their patients, as that is diametrically opposed to their mission of saving lives and curing disease. This type of headline is clickbait of the most nefarious variety, as it preys on peoples' hopes for good health (Affelt, 2017).

There are several helpful research tools that librarians can use when assisting patrons with medical research. Health-newsreview.org is a website that reviews news coverage of drugs, medical devices, vitamins and nutritional supplements, testing procedures, dietary recommendations, surgical procedures, and psychotherapy/mental health interventions (HealthNewsReview.org, n.d.). They assign a score of "satisfactory," "unsatisfactory," or "nonapplicable" by using a list of 10 elements that they require all health care news stories to contain. They then post the stories on their website, along with their review of the claims and the assigned score. The website also contains lists of credible new sites and links to industry experts and other organizations that evaluate health-care news (HealthNewsReview.org, n.d.).

NHS Behind the Headlines is a UK-based site that discusses research studies in detail (https://www.nhs.uk/news/). The site contains clickable lists of headlines which contain in-depth analysis featuring a summary of the research, including where it was reported, the type of study that was performed, and the characteristics of the data used, including where it was obtained and who the subjects were. It features a general summary of the raw testing results along with the interpretations of the researchers and scientists. Each study ends with a conclusion and critical analysis of the findings along with interpretation. Links to both the popular and academic press reports as well as the underlying data are provided (Affelt, 2017).

There are also fact-checking sites that are dedicated to evaluating information online and determining their truthfulness and accuracy. Snopes.com (www.snopes.com) began as an "urban legends" site and has evolved to fact-check many different categories of online information. Snopes.com is particularly reliable because of its transparency – the methodology used is clearly stated and their topic selection is based upon user input as well as a partnership with Facebook in which Snopes investigates both trending topics and items flagged by Facebook users. Snopes employs an extensive rating system in which information items are coded with labels ranging from true or false (or mostly true or false) to outdated, unproven, and scam (https://www.snopes.com/about-snopes/).

Politifact (www.politifact.com) assesses statements made by public officials using their "Truth-O-Meter," which has a scale ranging from true or false (or mostly true or false) to "pants on fire." Their evaluation criteria includes literal truthfulness, statements subject to interpretation, and evidence presented (Holan, 2018).

The Annenberg Public Policy Center of the University of Pennsylvania developed Factcheck.org (www.factcheck.org) in order to serve as a "consumer advocate" for voters while simultaneously trying to "reduce the level of deception and confusion in US politics" (FactCheck.org, 2018). Factcheck.org monitors the accuracy of statements by "major US political players," and is unique in that they not only review online information, but also speeches, TV ads, debate statements, and press releases.

*The Washington Post* Fact Checker (https://www.washingtonpost.com/news/fact-checker) is run by journalist Glenn Kessler and is user-driven; readers send statements for evaluation to a central email address and those that are chosen are subject to *The Post's* "Pinocchio Test" (Kessler, 2013). Statements that play a little loose and fast with the truth are given One Pinocchio. Statements that are misleading or have significant omissions or exaggerations merit Two Pinocchios. Mostly false statements with significant errors fit the Three Pinocchios category, and "whoppers" get Four Pinocchios. In December, 2018, *The Post* added a new category, "The Bottomless Pinocchio." This dubious distinction is awarded to claims with three or four Pinocchios which were repeated at least 20 times. *The Post* also awards statements that contain "the truth, the whole truth, and nothing but the truth," with their coveted "Geppetto Checkmark," named for the kindly woodcarver who stoicly endured the puppet Pinocchio's fibs and antics.

What about the old-fashioned way? We can rely on traditional librarianship skills in order to make these determinations either independently of or in addition to the safeguards listed in the guides discussed above. If you have a hard time finding information on a particular claim or news story that you are evaluating, you can try doing a search in Google by entering keywords for the story details, followed by additional terms such as "myth," "hoax," "scam," "false," "conspiracy," "clickbait," and "junk science." This technique might help you to uncover stories that debunk the claims in your article of interest. Also, read the comments section at the bottom of the article in question. Oftentimes commenters will post that an article has been debunked, along with a link to the backup reference (Affelt, 2017).

The pervasiveness of fake news has led to some unique challenges for librarians at the reference desk. While we have always been required to check out own biases at the door when performing reference service, the current climate has made it more difficult, as ignorance and skepticism rear their heads in equal amounts. By using these evaluated source lists and fake news red flag checklists, and providing them to patrons in order to enhance the credibility of our research when needed, we are better able to prove our objectivity. But what do we do when a patron insists that their research come from a source of their choosing? In these cases, as well, the IFLA and Zimdars documents can go a long way toward educating our patrons in practices of sound research (Affelt, 2017). Additionally, the American Library Association (ALA) and the Center for News Literacy at Stony Brook University are producing a six-month pilot program to train librarians to help patrons to become more news and media savvy. After a rigorous application process, five public libraries were chosen for the inaugural cohort, who will learn how to better identify fake news and produce public programs on information literacy (American Libraries, 2018).

*Library Journal* offers an online course for public, academic, and special librarians, "Fighting Fake News." The course equips librarians with tools for educating students and patrons in media literacy, with emphasis on communicating the importance of vetting news content and sources (*Library Journal*, 2017).

Librarians at the University of Michigan have responded to the "marked increase in the online dissemination of intentionally false information" by partnering with the UM College of Literature, Science, and the Arts to offer a course, "Fake News, Lies, and Propaganda: How to Sort Fact from Fiction." Going beyond basic media literacy, the course seeks to equip students in finding credible statistics, confronting bias, interpreting news, dissecting news graphs, and the pros and cons of social media news feeds (Michigan News, 2017).

Educators and journalists have long been seen as natural allies of librarian and information professionals. We stand shoulder to shoulder in the quest for finding credible information from high-quality sources and in the education of and assistance to others in doing the same. We are also held accountable to very similar professional standards – an accountability for accuracy, a responsibility for viewing all angles of a problem or challenge before drawing absolute conclusions, and a willingness to be forthcoming with regard to admission and correction of errors (Banks, 2016). To that end, in January of 2017, Reuters editor in chief Steve Adler took the unusual step of issuing a message to staff entitled, "Covering Trump the Reuters Way" (Reuters.com, 2017). Interestingly, it includes several tenets that are a direct part of the mission of librarianship. The following are among its directives:

- Cover what matters in people's lives and provide them the facts they need to make better decisions.
- Become ever-more resourceful: If one door to information closes, open another one.
- "What we have are sources" (Reuters.com, 2017).
- Learn about peoples' lives, what they think, and what helps and hurts them (great advice when developing library programming!).
- Keep Thomson Reuters Trust Principles close at hand ("integrity, independence, and freedom from bias") (Reuters.com, 2017).

Other precepts in the memo, such as the importance of being "intrepid and unbiased," admitting when we don't know something, valuing speed but not haste, and undertaking further investigation into issues that we are not 100% sure about (Reuters.com, 2017), would read like a list of "Characteristics of a Great Reference Librarian."

In order to train the next generation of journalists, the Dallas Public Library has partnered with *The Dallas Morning News* to offer "Storytellers Without Borders," an 8-week program for high school students in which they are mentored in reporting skills by journalists and in the use of research databases by librarians (Banks, 2016). The library portion of the program also includes instruction in multimedia editing tools. The ultimate goal is for the students to learn how to create content that is not only highly credible but also engaging and reflective of the socioeconomic and cultural diversity of the city (Banks, 2016). Upon completion of the program, the students' stories are then presented at the Dallas Book Festival.

What is trustworthy news? According to The Trust Project (https://thetrustproject.org/), it is news that is "accurate, accountable, and ethically produced" (The Trust Project, 2017a). It is easy to understand that definition, but in order to clarify its meaning in relation to actual journalistic practice, Sally Lehrman, director of the journalism ethics program at Santa Clara University, partnered with over 75 media organizations to combine efforts to define and identify credibility and quality in reporting, as well as promote transparency (The Trust Project, 2017b). Driven by interviews with news consumers and their stated values and beliefs, The Trust Project developed "The Trust Indicators," a set of questions to be answered by media outlets. They include disclosure of (The Trust Project, 2017a):

- Best practices regarding ethics, commitments to diversity, and accuracy
- Funding
- Author information
- Original sources of citations and references
- The reporting process and methodology

They also promote labeling of stories in order to distinguish opinion pieces and advertisements from hard news. The Trust Project also offers an alternative to the commonly used approaches of trying to label or remove fake news. Instead, they focus on promoting quality content, believing that "by focusing on reading and sharing news with integrity behind it, we can lessen the power of misinformation and stop its spread" (The Trust Project, 2017a). Not only are news organizations able to display the Trust indicators, but also, social media platforms like Facebook and Twitter and search engines such as Google and Bing are implementing a tagging system that allows them to either integrate the Trust indicators into their algorithms or to actually display them (The Trust Project, 2017a).

Given the current media climate and its ever-changing landscape of real and fake news, obtaining and honing information literacy skills has morphed into what will require a lifelong process of learning that needs to be constantly reassessed and tweaked. If we are to have an informed citizenry of critical thinkers, whether they are elementary school students using the library for the first time or university scholars conducting doctoral research, or senior citizens reading the daily news, we, as librarians, are going to have to continually keep abreast of any changes or new techniques that are being used to undermine quality content and share that information as much as we can. A one-day workshop on the CRAAP test isn't going to be enough. Brian Sullivan and Karen Porter of Alfred University believe that it is possible to transform those quick-and-dirty "spotting fake news" seminars in to an ongoing educational process where students encounter librarians "the more times, the better" (Sullivan & Porter, 2016). Ideally, these inter-actions would include multiple five-minute minilessons, one-on-one appointments with the librarian, topical sessions on concepts such as the characteristics of different types of sources, how to distinguish academic literature from popular press, and citation formatting (Sullivan & Porter, 2016). Sullivan and Porter's recommendations are meant to be applied in a university setting, but they work in any type of library. In an interesting twist on identifying fake news, instead of having students look for high-quality sources, which should be easy after the first few information literacy lessons, Sullivan and Porter distribute an assignment in which students are tasked with finding the "worst, most unreliable source on a sociological topic" (Sullivan & Porter, 2016). This is a great exercise that we should all try, for it just may be that the easiest way to spot fake news is to actively look for it.

# 5

# FAKE NEWS IN THE FIELD: LIBRARY SCHOOLS AND LIBRARIES

If librarians are going to take up the fight against fake news, it is imperative that they emerge from library school well armed with the proper knowledge and tools that they need to bring to the battle. This chapter takes a look at how information literacy skills and applications are being taught in library schools, and how that knowledge is being applied on the front lines by librarians at libraries.

As the problem of fake news continues to evolve, it is critical that LIS programs continually adjust their course offerings so that their graduates are well prepared to practice and model the tenets of sound information literacy once they are working in the field. Interestingly, of the 217 university, community college, high school, and public librarians questioned as part of a 2016 ProQuest survey of perceptions of information literacy, 90.8% of respondents stated that they believe that "one-on-one, in-person research consultations" are critical to helping users gain or improve information literacy skills (ProQuest, 2016). This statistic underscores the importance of the reference interview. Reference interviewing is one of the hallmarks of LIS programs, and it is usually one of the first courses taken in the program. Almost from day one, we learn how to ask the right questions of our constituents in order to get at the real question and to find out what information is really needed. As most librarians can attest, the question asked or problem presented is rarely what the requestor really needs to know. It is important to listen carefully, ask open-ended questions in order to receive clarification, repeat information back to the client in order to ensure that the query is fully understood, and depending on the complexity of the project, follow up repeatedly with updates of your progress in order to ensure that the research is going in the right direction and that the information and data you are using are on point (The State Library of Iowa, n.d.).

Dr Joyce Valenza, Assistant Professor at Rutgers University School of Communication and Information, believes that while library schools have always had the responsibility of equipping students with the necessary skills required to make sound information literacy decisions, new techniques and less-traditional resources should now be included to prepare practitioners for the current climate (Valenza, 2018). Social media companies are trying to stop the creation and dissemination of fake news. Valenza takes a different approach, stating, "The Internet is not going to change; we have to change." She believes that school librarians should help students curate content feeds containing articles from diverse and credible sources, rather than first going to social media for news (Valenza, 2018). More broadly, she suggests reviewing journalists' codes of ethics in order to understand the components of sound reporting practices, along with becoming familiar with news literacy vocabulary. Words such as "filter bubble," "virality," and "herding phenomenon," among others, can help librarians in efforts to explain credibility (Valenza, 2016). Her focus is a shift from trying to snuff out fake news to understanding more about it and creating viable alternatives.

Amy Gazaleh is the librarian at Hightstown High School, serving a student population of 1,600 in Hightstown, New Jersey. Gazaleh uses the CRAAP test as a tool when teaching evaluation of information. Interestingly, she also instructs students in the ethical use of information. She develops her curriculum with classroom teachers, customizing lessons to meet specific needs, ranging from plagiarism awareness and citation skills to advanced search technique and web site evaluation. Refreshingly, she does not see fake news as a major problem for high school students. She believes that if information literacy becomes ingrained in the culture of the school, and is emphasized from the top down, students cultivate and retain good information literacy habits. She also believes that students must be given reasons why it is important to use quality sources so that they understand the importance of "getting it right." With regard to library schools, Gazaleh stated that "the single most potentially impactful thing they could do is to increase outreach to and education for school administrators and boards of education about the strong connection between information literacy skills and college and career success" (Gazaleh, 2018). This is an interesting argument for adequate staffing, funding, and utilization of school libraries, and is supported by academic research. For example, a study at the Georgia State University Library found that students who used library resources such as research clinics had higher first-term grade point averages than their nonlibrary using peers (Kot & Jones, 2015). Similarly, Mark S. Thompson of Middlesex County College found that librarian/faculty collaboration in developing information literacy and critical thinking skills lessons led to improved student work and better preparation for coursework at four-year institutions (Thompson, 2013).

At the University at Albany, Associate Librarian for Social Welfare Elaine Lasda, and Information Literacy Librarian Kelsey O'Brien advocate for a values-based approach to helping students determine quality information and sources. For example, in teaching background research skills, Lasda believes that librarians should partner with other professions who share our dedication to information literacy and together bring a unified message with one voice (Lasda, 2018). She also uses an unconventional exercise in order to teach source evaluation; one of the assignments in the resource use and evaluation class that she teaches involves having students investigate a biased Internet source in order "to help drive home the point that not everything in PDF format is original, scholarly research." Further, as curriculum in the social welfare program evolves, Lasda foresees a greater reliance on popular press, traditional news, and policy papers rather than academic literature. She believes that this shift will precipitate a need for greater emphasis on teaching critical consideration of how to evaluate sources in information literacy courses (Lasda, 2018).

O'Brien believes that librarians should teach students to "value truth and expertise over expediency," and encourage them to "self-reflect, check their own biases, ask questions, engage with a variety of perspectives, and back their claims with evidence and expertise" (O'Brien, 2018). She also emphasizes the role of students as content creators, since because of social media, "they are constantly posting, sharing, and remixing information (and potentially misinformation)" (O'Brien, 2018). Regarding the CRAAP test, O'Brien and her colleagues added two additional considerations to the list: filter bubbles, (which result when search engines formulate results based on previous searches and websites visited, so that no two Internet searches ever reveal the exact same result lists (Pariser, 2012)), and confirmation bias ("the tendency to process information by looking for, or interpreting, information that is consistent with one's existing beliefs" (Casad, 2016)). Their goal in adding these two additional areas is to "encourage students to reflect on their own feelings and behaviors, rather than simply checking off boxes for what makes a 'good' source" (O'Brien, 2018).

O'Brien also worked with University at Albany colleagues to create the "Metaliteracy Badging System" (https://metal-iteracy.org/ml-in-practice/metaliteracy-badging/). This program consists of a series of exercises ranging from "quests" (lowest level) to "challenges" (next level up and composed of two or more quests). The individual exercises are designed to be incorporated into different courses, with each exercise having a written assignment associated with it that is assessed by the course instructor. While most instructors pick and choose selective exercises which correlate to their course objectives, there are four complete information literacy badges that can be earned: Master Evaluator, Producer & Collaborator, Digital Citizen, and Empowered Learner, with over 2,500 students of the University at Albany having completed at least one of the exercises (Jacobson, 2018). Each submission toward badge credit is reviewed by an educator, and revisions are usually required. Finally, students can become eligible for the "Ultimate Metaliteracy Badge," which denotes "extensive learning involving knowledge, reflection, self-awareness, and increased abilities" (Metaliteracy, n.d.).

In one of the exercises in the badging system, "Speaking Out," learners read about an incident in which inaccurate information in a Wikipedia entry led to a former aide to Robert Kennedy becoming falsely implicated in the Kennedy assassinations. They are then asked to "reflect on their own experiences with receiving and sharing misinformation, considering both the affective implications (how the experience made them feel), along with cognitive considerations (what strategies might they use to discern misinformation?)" (O'Brien, 2018). Further, students in a political science course were tasked with creating content for a Metaliteracy quest that was aligned with the course topics (O'Brien, 2018). These students then presented their quests to the class. In creating the content, these students gained a broader understanding of the underlying learning objectives of the badging system.

Lasda and O'Brien also believe that library schools have the opportunity to play a more prominent role in the education of future librarians so that they will be better prepared for future challenges surrounding information literacy. Lasda advocates for a focus on more web-based metadata and sources. For example, she sees a need for instruction in reading html metadata, understanding URL components, and awareness of common web hoaxes. She also believes that if library school curriculums included more emphasis on understanding how information literacy issues have evolved over time, "the context of how we got where we are in today's information landscape will enable librarians to take a more informed approach to handling the various situations that could arise as a result of a patron's acceptance of fake news as fact" (Lasda, 2018).

O'Brien sees a need for more higher level instruction in library schools regarding social networks, which, in her experience, have sometimes been seen by library school faculty as something to discount when conducting research. Instead of instructing students to avoid social media and web-based search engines and their results, O'Brien believes that library schools should prepare future librarians so that they "have a better understanding of the ways in which information is distributed and ranked online " (O'Brien, 2018). Arming students with intelligence regarding how search engine result lists are compiled and how the search engines themselves can be best used in order to uncover the most on-point, relevant results for each type of research query could go a long way toward helping them to position themselves as experts in these tools in their future work as professional librarians.

According to research conducted by the Pew Research Center, public libraries are seen as one of the most trustworthy institutions in America, with 77% of respondents in a Pew survey stating that they believe libraries are "essential to providing resources they can trust" (Alvarez, 2017). In tandem, around 70% of Americans believe that fake news is a major problem in the United States (Statista, 2018). Taken together, those statistics mandate that public librarians use their positions of trust to become part of the solution to the problem of fake news. As Barbara Alvarez states in *Public Libraries Online*, fake news can only exist if there is an absence of information and literacy, and it is imperative that librarians serve as "partners, educators, and community champions" and seize the opportunity to "teach information and media literacy," and "reframe ideas about navigating the Internet" (Alvarez, 2017). She lists the following activities as essential pieces of the credible news puzzle (Alvarez, 2017):

- Urge patrons to question the information they encounter.
- Walk patrons through the process of finding the information they need, even when answering their reference questions.
- Help patrons to use library databases and tools in order to find the information they need, rather than defaulting to always using Google.

- Provide resources and trainings regarding information evaluation.
- Encourage patrons to think critically about "sources, domain names, pop-up ads, and other indications about source credibility" (Alvarez, 2017).
- Offer lists of nonpartisan news sources.

American public libraries have responded to the challenge of combating fake news swiftly and with verve. A Google search on October 26, 2018 for "public library fake news program" lists initiatives at libraries from across the country. I was surprised and delighted to see information from seemingly disparate cities such as Wausau, Wisconsin, San Diego, Huntsville, Alabama, and Bellingham, Washington appear on my first page of results. This widespread penetration from all over the United States made me wonder if fake news is uniquely a US issue. To that end, I contacted Christina de Castell, Chief Librarian of Vancouver Public Library in Vancouver, British Columbia, Canada, to gain perspective on the impact of fake news on public libraries in Canada.

de Castell had a wonderful comment in response to a question I asked her about her personal encounters with fake news. She stated that the most common fake news that she hears (and I am certain most public librarians can relate to this) is a viewpoint most often held by people who don't use public libraries: that public libraries are not used. "Then they come for a tour and learn that 5,000 people visit our central library every day, proving this idea they've formed may itself have come from fake news" (de Castell, 2018). I asked de Castell to discuss the issue of fake news and its impact on the daily work of librarians, and what follows are her comments about this issue in her own library and in other libraries across Canada.

"In my former role as a director responsible for our collections, I had a conversation with our selections staff about fake news and false information in the context of science and health books. In Vancouver, we accept suggestions from the public for books we should buy. Our selections staff struggle with suggestions to buy books that present false information as true and the idea that libraries could further the spread of lies. I believe in freedom of information and that it's important not to censor; however, I also think it's critical in this environment that the information libraries provide can be trusted. This means that buying a book with clearly false information presented as fact should not be part of our library's practices; however, when the book is presented as opinion or discussion of opinions, we should consider it. These are tough choices, but I believe we have a responsibility to not actively spread misinformation.

Our public programming in Vancouver includes fake news as part of our digital literacy curriculum, and libraries across Canada offer programs on media and information literacy using fake news as part of the education.

Since I don't spend a lot of time on reference services, I also asked for input from our library staff and across Canada. Several commented that in reference services, it's health information that seems to come up most often, and that otherwise, they are rarely asked about fake news. Here are some of the stories and comments about how fake news is affecting library patrons in Canada."

## OTTAWA PUBLIC LIBRARY

"The proliferation of fake news means that we have to be especially careful in doing research for library customers, in addition to educating others on media literacy. Oftentimes, the customers we help lack the necessary information literacy skills to evaluate content on the web. We typically see this occurring more with older adults who become overwhelmed with the huge array of online news sources and often, the Internet itself. While assisting customers with their online research we usually find many unreliable or misleading sources. We explain why they are not ideal sources (biased, lack of citations, unreliable source/author, etc.) and show the customer how to identify them.

In our work, we've found that students in particular have heard the term fake news but don't always understand what it means in relation to web searching and looking for credible information. In meeting with students, we endeavor to include education on what is fake news and how to determine if an item is fake news when teaching students research skills/techniques. For example, in a presentation one staff member did for 8th graders at a local school, she used IFLA's statement on fake news as a teaching tool for students and then had them visit some preselected web sites to determine if the news was true or false. Discussions of satire, sources, and the importance of reading beyond ensued."

## VANCOUVER PUBLIC LIBRARY

"Just this week, a regular patron spoke with me about the recent decriminalization of marijuana in Canada and stated that he had heard that break-and-enter crime statistics had increased 200% in Colorado since the drug was legalized there. Since the transaction, I have followed up to possibly discuss this with the patron if he inquires again. I found no related statistic nearly as high as what he conveyed."

## SURREY PUBLIC LIBRARY

"The main way fake news affects librarians is in selections. Librarians receive requests for materials that are misinformation/opinion pieces sold as nonfiction, and this sometimes presents a dilemma for the selector, who usually does not want the item, but does as we want the library to represent views of our community with the exception of hate speech. The committee said they grapple with ordering requested inaccurate health information (e.g. Dr Oz books) more often than fake news, but there are requests for political books with very few real sources. Earlier this year, a staff member found a self-published book of Holocaust denial in the library, which was removed. Its sources cited were URLs from Google searches, which of course, found supporting material for the author's denial of Holocaust."

"Our patrons occasionally share 'fake news' within the library, but do not (or very rarely do) approach us with questions about whether sources of news are reliable article. Among librarians surveyed at ISC, only two reported Information Service Desk interactions around fake news, and patrons in these interactions were not consulting but directing Info Desk Staff.

(1) A patron told a staff member to watch a video about how the world was flat.
(2) Another told me that Noah's ark is all over the CNN."

"Some librarians described the issue as not that fake news directly involved in our daily work, but the issue is how some patrons treat our diverse staff members. Staff of visible minorities do experience hate speech and sometimes patrons cite fake news in the abuse; however, whether or not fake news causes the patron to speak this way, or the patron is using fake news to justify already firm beliefs, is another question. The feeling of staff is that hate speech against visible minorities is more frequent than before, but we have not done any analysis of this."


## MISSISSAUGA PUBLIC LIBRARY

Laura Kaminker, Mississauga Library – "In my experience working with teens in the library, our adolescent customers – the ones who are involved in the library, who tend to be very high achievers – are very aware that many stories they hear are not factual. Before the expression 'fake news' gained currency, they would use the expressions 'urban legends' or 'conspiracy theories' to describe the same phenomena. They would discuss, search on their phones, then discuss more, comparing sources. They would regularly debate the veracity of various sources – but they were all very clear that there was a possibility that any given source could not be trusted. They demonstrated a high degree of critical thinking."


## OSHAWA PUBLIC LIBRARY LIBRARIAN

"I was working at the reference desk when I heard a young male holler: 'Oh snap! Toni Braxton died!' I remember thinking that was unusual because I had browsed my news sources earlier that day and read no such story. I decided to do a quick fact that and found that Toni Braxton had not died (here I used a variety of methods including: checking Toni Braxton's personal website to see if anything was mentioned about her death, my Google news feed which has celebrity coverage and snopes.com fact-checking site which declared the story to be false.) After finding this information I went over to the patron who had made the statement and mentioned to him that I had looked into Toni Braxton and was sure she was still alive. We looked at the source of the information he had and I found it to be a questionable news site" (de Castell, 2018).

I also asked de Castell to address some additional questions regarding fake news; this is the text of our conversation:

**What do you think librarians can do in the fight against fake news? Do you think there are new skills that we need to learn, or do you see it more as a shift of existing skills to a new area? Please describe those skills whether they are new or existing.**

The critical thinking skills and education on evaluating sources that we have as librarians are absolutely valid in the digital and social media environment. We've learned about evaluating research studies, we understand following up on sources of information, we know the role of bibliographies and citations, and we've learned about literature reviews. We've also thought about issues of freedom of information and censorship, so most of us are likely to reflect carefully about our actions before we take them.

As far as what we can do, we can offer courses and incorporate teaching evaluation of sources in our public programming and our information services. Our first responsibility is to ensure that everyone in the library understands the problem and has the skills to evaluate fake news, so we need to make sure we're teaching each other and taking responsibility for investigating the truth of the information that we share personally.

IFLA created an infographic about evaluating news, and we can help spread tools like that one to our communities, to encourage people to start thinking and learning.

**What should librarians do when patrons insist that fake news is real?**

This is tricky. Every question is valid, and we have to treat our patrons with respect. It's worth offering an alternative source. If they're a regular patron, coming back to them at another time to see whether they might be interested in learning about how to evaluate news could be an option. We want people to know they can come to us with their questions, so it's not likely to be a good choice to argue about fake news with a patron.

**Do you think it is possible for social media platforms to stop the spread of fake news? If so, what steps do you think they can take to accomplish this?**

I think it's possible for social media platforms to give people the tools to stop the spread. So far, I don't think technology is ready for doing it alone.

**What should library schools be doing to prepare the next generation of librarians to be able to fight fake news?**

Library schools need to keep on offering courses that teach the skills for evaluating information, with a focus on the digital environment and social media. We also need to learn how to provide effective, engaging instruction to patrons on this topic. When we're discussing our professional values, we're going to need to spend more time talking about our role in selecting materials and how our values play out in that context because it's much easier to publish now, both in print and digitally, and as a result we're seeing many more books that contain false information.

**What future challenges do you see in the fight against fake news?**

Artificial intelligence has the potential to improve the quality of the writing in fake content, so we could have increasing material that seems credible and isn't real. It may also offer us systems that can do a better job of evaluating the quality and accuracy of information, so perhaps these two advancements will be concurrent, but one could also overtake the other. Where the investment goes will certainly affect that (de Castell, 2018).

Finally, one additional activity, which is less obvious but just as critical for public libraries to carry out in efforts to combat fake news, according to Alvarez, is advocacy. Since public libraries provide credible information from high-quality sources, whether they be newspapers, magazines, books, or digital resources, it is imperative that community members visit the library so that they can procure them from us. Going beyond occasional marketing, Alvarez believes that advocacy by librarians is "essentially part of the job description," and is "nonnegotiable," with an information-literate public "depending on it" (Alvarez, 2017).

The ProQuest survey also found that only 25.4% of librarians surveyed believe that their library supports information literacy instruction needs as much as it should (ProQuest, 2016). This is yet another statistic reinforcing the need for advocacy by librarians within their communities and institutions. LIS schools need to ensure that future librarians have the skills to do this by bolstering their marketing classes and even teaching sales techniques so that librarians are not only able to "sell" their constituents on the need for high-quality, citable information from reliable sources, but also reinforce the belief that the library is the best place to find them.

So how do we advocate for use of public libraries? Encouraging people to apply for and renew their library cards is a start. Once that step is taken, marketing and outreach efforts can be deployed to extol the benefits of using the library facilities and participating in its programs. Finally, as is true with most advocacy efforts, relationship-building is critical. Libraries need to constantly position themselves as the institutions with the best information resources and the most capable staff who can assist citizens in the use of those resources. In short, all public library advocacy efforts should be working toward the goal of positioning the library as the place that "community members can trust," with librarians as "people they can believe in" (Alvarez, 2017).

# 6

# THE FUTURE OF FAKE NEWS: THE VIEW FROM HERE

When the Buggles sang of the end of radio in the very first music video shown on MTV in 1981, they predicted that once the video music format was ushered in, recorded music as we knew it would be forever changed. For quite some time now, I have characterized Internet video, whether it is a news report or sheer entertainment, as "the genie in the bottle." I believe that once video takes off as the preferred information format, just as the Buggles sang way back when, "we can't rewind, we've gone too far." If video is the preferred format, we will never go back to text as the predominant format.

It can be argued that the very first viral video was created on March 3, 1991, when Rodney King was filmed being beaten by members of the Los Angeles Police Department during an arrest for speeding. A bystander on a nearby balcony took the footage with a Sony camcorder, and it was soon seen over and over again on television sets all over the world. Initially, civil rights leaders believed that the images would transform public opinion regarding race and the criminal justice system; at that time, the video medium was widely believed to be objective. However, the officers were acquitted the following year (Zelizer, 2017). The reasons for that acquittal have been debated ever since (and a switch of trial venue to conservative Simi County played a large role), but one thing is for certain: the possibility of the video being fabricated was not a consideration. No one would have dreamed of accusing Rodney King of being a "crisis actor," in order to drum up sympathy for the cause, as they did of David Hogg in the Parkland school shooting. Obviously, times have changed, along with our attitudes toward videos, fake and real.

Long before the fake news era, information in video format has presented a challenge for librarians at the reference desk. When requestors come to us, they are typically looking for information from the past; it is rare that a research request is for breaking news. As video takes off, whether it is a video from two days ago, two weeks ago, or two years ago, we will be asked to find it. In 2016 alone, over 8 billion videos were watched every day on Facebook (Goldman, 2016). Fast-forward five years, and imagine a requestor asking the librarian to find one of those videos. As of today, we do not have a good way to do that. Facebook states that they archive all videos, but what periodicity of history will be available? And even if the archive is extensive, as of right now, there isn't a good way to find historical videos.

Since projects that are tasked to librarians usually involve looking to past activity in order to find answers and source material, as of now, they usually do not involve looking for video. Video search engines at this point are a long way away from being able to locate not only the actual videos themselves but also all of the metadata, indexing, transcripts, and graphical images that go along with them. However, when Facebook EMEA VP Nicola Mendelsohn stated that Facebook will be "all video" in five years, and remarked that text has been declining every year, and that Facebook users now view videos 8 billion times per day, up from 1 billion a year ago, it became apparent that Facebook thinks video will kill off text, sooner rather than later (Zillman, 2016). Not only is Facebook a huge influencer of news content (Pew Research Center reports that six-in-ten online millennials get political news on Facebook in any given week, "a much larger percentage than turn to any other news source") (Mitchell, Gottfried, & Matsa, 2015) but also they are monetarily incentivizing video production by news companies, according to an April 2016 report in *BuzzFeed*, which stated that Facebook pays news organizations $250K for a three-month stint of posting 20 videos per month (Kantrowitz, 2016). Also, according to a document reviewed by *The Wall Street Journal*, Facebook awarded a $3.03 million contract to *The New York Times* for one year of broadcasting live (Perlberg & Seetharaman, 2016). How does that bode for the future of text, and more importantly, for the future of research sources used by librarians at the reference desk? If money talks, text might walk, and librarians will be left to find individual archival videos in a vast ocean of content. Regardless, it seems that Facebook is forcing our hand, and in the not-too-distant future, librarians will need to focus on finding an effective method of searching archival videos that results in efficient retrieval.

This challenge seems daunting enough in and of itself, but imagine the havoc that fake news in video form could wreck. In July 2017, a team of computer scientists from the University of Washington used audio clips and algorithms programmed to manipulate mouth movements in order to produce a lip-synced video of Barack Obama (Miller, 2017). The result was so lifelike that former Bush and Obama special adviser on technology and cyber security David Edelman thought it was real. "Now, I wrote speeches for the guy.

I know him. I cannot tell the difference between the real and the fake. That's the power of the technology we're talking about," he stated (Nott, 2018).

While this exercise was not completely new, as Face2Face, a technology developed by researchers at Stanford University can create similar videos by manipulating a face on a video image according to the movements of a different face on a webcam (Nott, 2018); it is novel in that it uses machine learning to link mouth shapes, pauses, head nods, and other expressions gleaned from existing video and allows for dubbing of new audio over those existing videos, creating a startlingly realistic product (Nott, 2018). Examples of the nefarious purposes for which this might be used include reordering words actually spoken by a subject in order to imply a different meaning, matching up videos of impersonators with actual audio of the real subject, and taking earlier videos of a subject and altering them to make it look like they were being said at a totally different point in time (Nott, 2018). It is a scary prospect to be sure, but we can take comfort in at least one limitation that the technology has, at least for now; the algorithm requires that a lot of existing footage of the subject exists in order to write the code. Therefore, it limits the scope of people who could potentially become victims of fake videos, but it also means that those most vulnerable to video manipulations are "figures of authority" and "people we trust" (Nott, 2018).

BuzzFeed founder and CEO Jonah Peretti wanted to create a PSA that would sound a clarion call regarding the future of fake news, which BuzzFeed characterized as "a slew of slick, easy-to-use, and eventually seamless technological tools for manipulating perception and falsifying reality, for which terms have already been coined – 'reality apathy,' 'automated laser phishing,' and 'human puppets'" (Mack,

2018). Peretti focused on fake video for the PSA because he believes that while people are starting to become more skeptical regarding textual information, they still easily fall prey to fake videos, with the conventional wisdom being that people think video is real because "video doesn't lie" (Mack, 2018). The resulting PSA featured manipulated and digitally altered footage of Barack Obama with audio voiced by Oscar award–winning screenwriter Jordan Peele. Peretti and Buzz-Feed video producer Jared Sosa used Adobe After Effects software and AI program FakeApp to paste Peele's mouth over Obama's and replace Obama's jawline with Peele's moving mouth. FakeApp was used to tweak the footage (Mack, 2018).

While there is a wide range of sophistication among fake videos, according to MIT Technology Review, basic digital face swaps, which involve swapping out video images and adding audio from an unrelated source, can be made by "anyone with a decent computer and a few hours to spare" (Knight, 2018b). OpenFaceSwap is a free, downloadable, face-switching program which can be rented for "a few cents per minute," using a cloud-based machine learning platform such as Paperspace. Once accessed, its algorithm analyzes two videos uploaded by the user, figures out how each face looks and moves, and then maps one onto the other (Knight, 2018b). OpenFaceSwap uses an artificial neural network, "the go-to tool in AI (artificial intelligence)" which is able to locate specific images out of sets of millions, along with synthesizing and manipulating these images (Knight, 2018b). Using a data compression mechanism, OpenFaceSwap decodes images, feeding encoded data for one image into the decoder for another. It then creates one face that mimics the other's expressions and movements. While the results can be extremely rudimentary, OpenFaceSwap is also able to blur edges and adjust color and light to make the new images look more realistic (Knight, 2018b). For audio swapping, a similar technology called Lyrebird can be used to recreate voices.

When fake video and fake audio are combined, dire consequences may result. For example, in April 2018, a purported BBC News clip on WhatsApp showed footage of missiles being fired while a broadcaster announced that parts of Frankfurt, Germany, had been destroyed (Knight, 2018b). The video was fake and was renounced by the BBC, but it portends a future where a fake video could possibly incite anything from a stock market crash to World War Three. Writing in *The Atlantic*, Franklin Foer cautions that when people look at something, they don't always see the same thing. If we live in a world where our eyes routinely deceive us, "We're not so far from the collapse of reality" (Foer, 2018). Since "it's natural to believe what one sees," altered or fabricated videos exploit that tendency, "creating new and understandable suspicions about everything we watch" (Foer, 2018).

Along with a concern about present and future reality, Brian Resnick of Vox believes that our past memories may also be manipulated by fake videos, which have the capability of creating false memories (Resnick, 2018). Just as we often remark that "we can't unsee it," about something we would have rather not viewed in the first place, researchers have found that the mind easily forms false memories, and that capability goes into overdrive on the Internet, as we have seen with fake news. As Joshua Rothman writes in *The New Yorker*, "It's not just that what we see can't be unseen. It's that, in our memories and imaginations, we keep seeing it" (Rothman, 2018). Fake videos "make planting false memories even easier" (Rothman, 2018). In 2010, *Slate* asked 1,000 people if they remembered seeing a fake photo of President Barack Obama shaking hands with former Iranian president Mahmoud Ahmadinejad. 21% replied that they remembered seeing the photo, and 25% stated that they remembered the event but couldn't recall the image (Rothman, 2018). Additional research by *Slate* found that fake photos provoked false memories in at least 15% of respondents, with 50% also stating that they believed the events in the fake photos actually took place. Finally, people were much more likely to state that they remembered a fake photo when it fit their political affiliation, causing researchers from California State University, Los Angeles, who partnered with *Slate* on the project, to conclude that "doctored photos can change the way we remember history" (Rothman, 2018). "When people lie or stretch the truth, sometimes that itself distorts their memory," according to psychologist Steven Frenda of Cal State LA. "So they will sometimes incorporate their lies or exaggerations into what it is to what they think they genuinely remember" (Rothman, 2018). The more we hear an idea, the more likely it is to become embedded into our memory, and, according to Frenda, we tend to forget the sources of information, making it possible to see a fake video from a non-credible news source and "misremember that you actually saw it on CNN" (Rothman, 2018). Fake videos are troubling in and of themselves, but consider how they could be used to substantiate textual fake news. In the future, we will be forced to not only evaluate and try to eliminate fake news in text form, but also, we will need to account for the fake videos that go along with it.

Lawmakers and intelligence officials refer to fake videos as "deepfakes." Claire Wardle of Harvard's Shorenstein Center defines deepfakes as "fabricated media produced using artificial intelligence...in which individuals appear to speak words and perform actions, which are not based on reality" (Wardle, 2018). How do we spot them? There are several techniques, which at least for now, can be used.

## THE EYES HAVE IT

In determining veracity of video, it is helpful to remember the old adage, "the eyes have it." In looking for qualities that might indicate tampering or false creation, the first telltale sign is whether or not the eyes blink. Human beings in real video recordings should blink at the ordinary rate of 17 blinks per minute. "AI-generated faces lack eye blinking function," according to Siwei Lyu, a computer scientist at the University at Albany (Johnson, 2018).

## PUT YOUR MONEY WHERE THE MOUTH IS

Mouth anomalies are some of the biggest deepfake giveaways, as tools that create deepfake videos still have a long way to go in generating realistic-looking mouths. According to image forensics expert Professor Hany Farid of Dartmouth College, they run into difficulties "to accurately render the teeth, tongue, and mouth interior" (Silverman, 2018).

## HOT BLOODED? CHECK IT AND SEE

If you are able to examine videos on a pixel level, you might be able to look for blood flow in the faces of the video subjects. If there isn't any blood flow, the footage may not be real (Pierson, 2018). Also, look for a pulse. People in fake videos might not really be alive.

## GO SLOW-MO

If you slow down a video and look at freeze-framed shots within it, you may uncover "temporal glitches that are introduced in manipulated video," according to Farid (Silverman, 2018). These often reveal themselves in the transition from frametoframe.

## REMEMBER THE OLD STANDBYS

Although the medium is different, evaluating a video for veracity still requires the same standards that we used when evaluating text. Just as the IFLA document admonished in Chapter 4, it is important to consider the source of the video, including the original creator and where it is now being found. Is someone claiming to be the creator? If so, what is their source? It is also important to consider the context. What if a video is real, but the accompanying online story is about something entirely different? This possibility requires that we also read the titles of the videos and any related text, using that information to conduct further research to ensure that the video is really depicting that which is stated.

If the abovementioned tips for spotting deepfakes do not seem very extensive or foolproof, it is because they are not. We desperately need new tools to be developed, along with other mechanisms that can be put into place in order to ensure that videos are real. Additionally, as with most nefarious activities, part of the challenge is to stay one step ahead of the deepfake creators. As Hany Farid predicts, "If you really want to fool the system, you will start building into the deepfake ways to break the forensic system," and even so, he warns that we are "decades away from having forensic technology that…(could) conclusively tell a real from a fake" (Matsakis, 2018). To that end, the US Department of Defense's Defense Advanced Research Projects Agency (DARPA) launched a contest in July of 2018 in which 10 teams from US and European universities competed to develop new video, image, and audio veracity tools. The teams were given 2–3 weeks to analyze fake videos, process data, and generate output to give to the National Institute of Standards and Technology, where work is being done to create algorithms that determine if videos are real or fake. The contest is part of a four-year "media forensics" program that "brings together researchers to design tools to detect video manipulations and provide details about how the fakery was done" (Silverman, 2018).

Horizon 2020 is a European Union program which has a goal of enabling "breakthroughs, discoveries, and world-firsts by taking great ideas from the lab to the market" (European Commission, n.d.). One of Horizon 2020's funded projects is a plugin for Chrome that can be used to debunk fake videos. The plugin, which was developed by InVID and is currently in open beta, allows a user to enter a URL for a video and have it analyzed by the plugin, which generates metadata (location, description, time) and allows for further exploration with suggestions such as reverse image searches and Twitter video search (Maack, 2017). It also contains tabs with additional features such as the ability to fragment videos into keyframes, enhance and explore keyframes and images with a magnifying glass, download metadata, and apply forensics filters (InVID Verification Plugin, 2018).

SurfSafe is a browser plugin created by Robhat Labs; the idea behind it, according to developer Ash Bhat, is to filter Internet content for falsehoods in real time, working behind the scenes in a similar way to antivirus software. "We want to scan your news feed for fake news as you browse," Bhat says (Lapowsky, 2018). Users can hover over images while Surf-Safe fact-checks information using over 100 trusted news sites and debunking sites like Snopes. It does this by assigning a unique digital fingerprint to every photo it encounters on its list of trusted sites. It does the same thing for each photo its users encounter while browsing the Internet. It then compares the two fingerprints in order to determine if they are the same, or "almost, but not precisely, the same" (Lapowsky, 2018). The algorithm learns by organizing the fingerprints according to which image was encountered first, since that image is most likely to be the original. Bhat's goal is similar to that of Mark Zuckerberg, in that his biggest concern is not the existence of fake news and videos but their ability to rapidly and widely spread. SurfSafe has a blind spot in that images that it has never encountered have an end result of being unmatched, even if they are fake, but since virality is Bhat's primary concern, he views this as benign (Lapowsky, 2018).

US Senators Mark Warner of Virginia and Marco Rubio of Florida have emerged as two of the lawmakers most concerned about the infiltration of fake videos into the world of fake news. Warner would like to amend the Communications Decency Act to hold social media companies accountable for fake videos and manipulated content on their platforms, stating that the platforms are "in the best place to identify and prevent this kind of content from being propagated" (Hawkins, 2018). Interestingly, he has recognized that a fine line exists between deepfakes and satire, entertainment, and parody, but that "courts already must make distinction between satire and defamation/libel" (Hawkins, 2018). In a 20-point policy paper, he writes that deepfakes could "usher in an unprecedented wave of false and defamatory content" (Hawkins, 2018). Rubio has yet to introduce any concrete proposals, but has expressed concern that there has been little or no preparation regarding the ability of fake news and videos to "sow instability and chaos in American politics" (Hawkins, 2018).

Politics aside, leading technology thought leaders have expressed disparate ideas regarding ways to parse out and stop the spread of fake videos, but one of the best ways comes from library and information science. Computer scientists typically define metadata as "data that provides information about other data" (Merriam-Webster, n.d.), but I usually describe it as "the term formally known as indexing." Most of us took an indexing and abstracting course in library school, and assignation of index terms is a key skill gleaned from that course. Basically, metadata are index terms, and if videos came with metadata, or indexing terms that describe them, those descriptors would be a key component in determining "when, where, and how" it was captured (*The Economist*, 2017b). First, they would identify a video as fake if its metadata did not match local conditions at the time it was supposedly filmed. An Internet conspiracy theory surrounding the Apollo 11 lunar landing illustrates how this would work. The hoax was created because photos of astronaut Buzz Aldrin's space suit reveal "odd-looking lighting...taken by some nitwits as evidence of fakery" (*The Economist*, 2017). Chip manufacturer NVIDIA set out to debunk this theory by using its chips to analyze the photos and simulate the bounce of light rays to show that the highlights in the pictures are actually reflected lunar sunlight (*The Economist*, 2017).

The Citizen Evidence Lab at Amnesty International uses several methods to verify videos and images of alleged human rights abuses. Since fighting these abuses is the crux of their mission, it is critical that they get this right. They use Google Earth to examine background landscapes and create metadata capturing when and where videos and images were created, and then they go a step further and use Wolfram Alpha to double-check historical weather conditions to ensure that they are consistent with those in the videos. Amnesty International reports that these techniques largely uncover not fake videos, but usually old videos that are being touted as a new atrocity (*The Economist*, 2017).

New forms of watermarking, which can be used to add a digital signature to images, also show great promise. Truepic is a startup that aims to produce verifiable, original digital photographs by taking uploaded photos with a smartphone app and storing them in a "cryptographic lockbox" (Rothman, 2018). After they ensure that the GPS, cell tower, and phone barometric pressure sensor data surrounding the photo matches, they run it through computer vision tests and enter it into the blockchain, a type of digital ledger that records every change made to documents (and could potentially be used to archive every change to a photo or video.) The Truepic photos are then shared on a special web page which verifies their authenticity (Rothman, 2018). Truepic is currently used by insurance companies to verify claims, with policyholders providing verified photos of everything from flooded basements to broken car windows, and by other industries in which there is a "trust gap": for example, construction workers in Kazakhstan use it to take "verified selfies" when punching the time clock. Truepic's CEO, Jeffrey McGregor, believes it also has potential applications in property rentals and online dating, with his ultimate goal being to incorporate the software into camera components so that "verification can begin the moment photons enter the lens" (Rothman, 2018).

Video recorders that digitally sign every video they create could also be combined with blockchain technology. Every device purchased would be listed in a public database, along with its digital access key, so that any video that device produced in the future would have that same digital signature, which could be traced back to a specific purchaser. This type of technology would create a two-tiered system for video production – videos that have a digital signature and are verifiably authentic, and those that do not. If nothing else, it would lend a high degree of confidence that signed videos are real (Lin, 2018).

Factom is a company that is harnessing technology to produce devices that ensure video authenticity. Factom has developed a product which analyzes chunks of videos for veracity, using blockchain technology to guarantee that streaming video entering Factom's cameras is authentic for whatever chunk of time that video resides there. The data are organized and instantly digitally signed, assuring that the video is real and was taken by the camera that digitally signed it (Martinez, 2018).

Although the development of new technologies that can be used to determine veracity of video will continue to grow over time, there is still the problem of video virality. Once the fake videos are created and shared, what course of action can be undertaken in order to try to one, delete the video, both real-time and historically, and two, prevent fake video virality going forward? Robert Chesney and Danielle Citron, law professors at the University of Texas and University of Maryland, respectively, describe the deepfake "worst case scenario," as "a world in which it becomes child's play to portray people as having done or said things they did not say or do" (Chesney & Citron, 2018). Lacking not only the technology needed to expose the fakes but also legal options for punishing and deterring their usage, Chesney and Citron envision a possible solution in "immutable authentification trails" (Chesney & Citron, 2018). While this is probably only a practical solution for high-profile individuals, these trails would compile a "life log," using a model in which one pays to have a third-party vendor track "movements, elec-tronic communications, in-person communications, and surrounding visual circumstances" (Chesney & Citron, 2018). The vendor would have agreements with media platforms which would allow for immediate debunking of deepfakes involving its clients. Obviously, the impact of such a system on personal privacy is grave; therefore, Chesney and Citron advocate for government regulation of these systems, with warrant requirements for acquisition of any of the data.

Chesney and Citron have also laid out possible legal and regulatory actions. Laws which ban the harmful aspects of deepfake technology while allowing beneficial ones (which is problematic since it requires proof of the creator's intent to deceive and harm) would probably be ultimately deemed unconstitutional, as two landmark US Supreme Court decisions, *New York Times* v. *Sullivan* in 1964 and *United States* v. *Alvarez* in 2012 allowed that false speech enjoys constitutional protection, and that falsity alone does not remove expression from First Amendment protection (Chesney & Citron, 2019, forthcoming). Regarding civil suits, it may be difficult for the plaintiff to prove the identity of the creator, or, given the global nature of online platforms and the deepfakes that are posted to them, the creator may be beyond the reach of the law (Chesney & Citron, 2019, forthcoming). Even if a civil suit is able to go forward, the plaintiffs usually need to pay for the legal fees, which can be prohibitive.

If a deepfake creator can be identified, there are several avenues for possible litigation. Videos in which copyright infringement can be proved are subject to monetary damages and mandatory removal procedures. Misappropriation of likeness for commercial gain, infliction of emotional distress, systemic harms (i.e., if the video sets off violence in a community), and defamation are other possible angles (Chesney & Citron, 2019, forthcoming). Chesney and Citron also believe that several criminal statues might apply to deepfake creation. Cyberstalking laws, laws against impersonation crimes, and incitement charges (i.e., in the case of a video inciting a riot) may be applicable (Chesney & Citron, 2019, forthcoming).

Lawsuits against online platforms are another consideration. Currently, the platforms are protected by Section 230 of the Communications Decency Act (CDA), which absolves the platforms from being considered as creators of the content, however defamatory or harmful. However, Chesney and Citron believe that an amendment to CDA Section 230, which would mandate that platforms take "reasonable steps" to ensure that the platforms were not being used for illegal actions, is a possibility (Chesney & Citron, 2019, forthcoming).

Chesney and Citron also see potential roles for three government agencies, the Federal Trade Commission (FTC), Federal Communications Commission (FCC), and the Federal Election Commission (FEC) in regulating deepfakes. If a deepfake could also be considered a form of advertising, it is possible that the FTC could become involved in its role of "protecting consumers from fraudulent advertising relating to 'food, drugs, devices, services, or cosmetics'" (Chesney & Citron, 2019, forthcoming). Although currently, according to Chesney and Citron, the FCC "appears to lack jurisdiction" over social media content, as attention to fake news grows greater as fake videos proliferate, the FCC may be motivated to reinterpret current rules or make new ones (Chesney & Citron, 2019, forthcoming). Finally, since the main focus of the FEC's current efforts has been to "increase transparency regarding sponsorship and funding for political advertising," it is possible that their transparency requirements could include "elements of attribution and accountability for content creators" (Chesney & Citron, 2019, forthcoming). If these creators make fake videos, they may be culpable.

Interestingly, the above fake news and fake video solutions involve a combination of market and government resources. Innovative companies are creating groundbreaking products that help to authenticate information at the same time that government resources exist to help the public at large. This gives me great hope that disparate groups of people will work together to improve the quality and integrity of Internet information in the future. A key component of all of the possible remedies is that they increase awareness of the fact that at a basic level, fake news and fake videos exist and are rampantly spread. The best-case scenario for us as librarians and information professionals is that widespread concern over fake news will facilitate a constant dialog among these wide-ranging groups of stakeholders. I believe that most people do want to harness information that is correct, and ideally, if the problem of fake news can be kept at the forefront, it might cause people to acquire the innate skepticism that we have as professionals working in the information field. If, when confronted with news, whether in text or video form, users first hit the pause button, then take the information through a veracity checklist, and then made a judgment after carefully considering all of the possibilities surrounding whether or not the information is real or fake, we will go a long way toward a more informed information-consuming public and democracy at large.

# CONCLUSION

*You have to believe in facts. Without facts, there is no basis for cooperation.*

– Former US President Barack Obama, speaking in Johannesburg, South Africa, at a celebration of the 100th anniversary of the birth of Nelson Mandela (National Public Radio, 2018)

The above-mentioned quote from Barack Obama underscores the reality that it is impossible to even begin to have a dialogue when there is no established common ground. Diplomacy is practiced when first, both parties understand the issues on the table. They usually agree on what these issues are; the challenge is in determining what each party wants so that there can be give and take, compromise, and mutual respect and understanding. If we can't agree on the basic facts and principles, all bets are off. As Obama joked in his speech, "If I say this is a podium and you say this is an elephant, it's going to be hard for us to cooperate" (National Public Radio, 2018). If basic fundamentals are in clear misalignment, the conversation has no way to evolve.

When former US Vice President Al Gore won the Nobel Peace Prize in 2007 for his work in education about and awareness of climate change, some wondered how that met the criteria of the award or how it qualified as working toward peace. However, as Gore continues to argue, extreme weather can lead to conflict and war. For example, massive drought caused by climate change can lead to agricultural collapses that create devastating conflict among populations competing for scarce resources. Gore and other leading scientists have sounded a clarion call for years that future wars will be waged over water, or the near depletion of it in major cities around the globe (CBS News, 2017b).

Recalling this debate made me wonder: will there be future wars waged over facts? Gore called global warming a "planetary emergency" (Barringer & Revkin, 2007). The creation, dissemination, and spread of fake news is also a planetary emergency, and one that is already causing wars, although as of right now, they are mostly ideological rather than physical. Perhaps a type of Nobel Peace Prize needs to be created and awarded in order to encourage the media to engage in the fight for high-quality, fully vetted news. How can we work toward that? What follows are a few ideas.

Canadian Senator Murray Sinclair once remarked, "Education is what got us in to this mess, and education will get us out" (Atleo, 2013). He said that in his role as Chair of the Truth and Reconciliation Commission, but the quote is often widely shared and used in many different contexts, since it is so applicable to many situations. I can't help but think of it but with a changeup – "News is what got us in to this mess, and news will get us out." The best thing that we can do to fight fake news is to advocate for quality news. What is needed is a type of "Good Housekeeping Seal of Approval" for news organizations, developed by an independent, highly qualified panel of recognized news industry leaders. In order to earn the seal, media outlets would need to meet and maintain a list of developed standards regarding sources and reporting.

A common list of standards for veracity of news is only valuable if people understand how to use it, and they will also need additional training in where to go to find these vetted sources. 31% of participants in a September 2017 Pew Research Center survey agreed that "getting training on how to use online resources to find trustworthy information would help them a lot in making decisions" (Horrigan, 2017). How will they receive this training? It is imperative that librarians take on this role, and it seems that we have a mandate; the same Pew survey found that libraries and librarians were the number one trusted providers of information sources (Horrigan, 2017). We even edged out healthcare providers this time, who were trusted by 39% of adults in comparison with 40% for librarians.

What about news whose creation and dissemination is completely beyond our control? That leads us to Facebook. It seems as though they dominate news headlines on a daily basis with a constantly changing solution to stopping the spread of fake news on the platform (From January 2017 to August 2018, there were over 1,500 headlines on Factiva that mention Facebook and "fake news"). In order to address these growing concerns, UK lawmakers drafted a report on fake news after a year-long investigation into misinformation on social media platforms. Among their recommendations were taxes, fines, and a call for "'clear legal liability' for tech companies to act against content that is deemed 'harmful and illegal'" (Gold, 2018). In response, Facebook Vice President for Policy Richard Allan stated, "We will work closely with the UK Government and Electoral Commission as we develop these new transparency tools" (Gold, 2018). Similarly, the French government announced that beginning in 2019, they will take the unprecedented step of studying Facebook's content moderation algorithms and processes, and that they will be given access to Facebook's content inclusion and exclusion policies (Kelly, 2018). French regulators will investigate "how flagging works, how Facebook identifies problematic content, how Facebook decides if it's problematic or not and what happens when Facebook takes down a post, a video, or an image," and will also look for signs of algorithmic bias (Dillet, 2018).

Perhaps what is needed is a radical solution: give up. It almost seems impossible for Facebook to stop the creation and spread of fake news, and Facebook's top executive in charge of eliminating misinformation on the platform admitted as much. In an interview for a *Frontline* episode on Facebook and fake news, Tessa Lyons, Product Manager for News Feed Integrity, stated, "You know, I came into this job asking myself: How long is it going to take us to solve this? And the answer is, this isn't a problem that you solve. It's a problem that you contain" (Jacoby & Bourg, 2018). So can Facebook contain fake news? Claire Wardle believes that Facebook simply does not have the vetting and editorial systems in place to do so (Solon, 2016). Maybe it is ok after all that they insist they are all technology company and not a news company. "For one thing, Facebook isn't wired for the nuanced process of deciding which news posts and pages are truth and which ones aren't" (Sullivan, 2018).

Since none of the Facebook fake news solutions have really seemed to do the trick, they could wave the white flag and institute a "click to agree" button at each log-in. Users would read a disclaimer stating that "We are not a media company. You may be viewing fake news, satire, pseudoscience, violent images, fake videos, doctored photos, and outright falsehoods. This is meant to be an entertaining and fun way to connect with friends and not an educational experience." They'd still sell ads; indeed, if memory serves, they seem to be unaffected by every scandal that breaks. After revelations such as the fact that Facebook allowed Cambridge Analytica to collect user data through a quiz app which was used to build voter profiles during the 2016 US presidential election, that they scanned users' photos and links sent via Facebook Messenger, and that they retained videos that users thought they had deleted (Jenkins, 2018), their user numbers continued to climb, and "the Facebook juggernaut marches on" (Frenkel & Roose, 2018).

Even after Facebook lost $120 billion in market value in a single day (July 26, 2018), it still remained the fifth most valuable company in American markets, and, aside from a few shareholders and public interest groups, there weren't any calls for Zuckerberg's resignation, which sometimes has happened at other companies experiencing a similar drop in stock price (Manjoo, 2018a). Zuckerberg is the "face" of Facebook; it is hard to imagine one without the other. Writing in *The New York Times* in November 2018, technology columnist Farhad Manjoo argued that Zuckerberg is "too big to fail" (Manjoo, 2018b). Facebook's current initiatives, such as hiring more fact-checkers and content reviewers and putting future projects on hold, may lead to stymied revenue growth, but since Zuckerberg's shares in the company have 10 times the voting power of ordinary shares, he has total dominance of the company's equity. Therefore, unlike other CEOs who have been fired following missteps that negatively impacted the bottom line, Zuckerberg is well equipped to withstand the financial fallout of implementing these necessary changes and, according to a Facebook executive interviewed by Manjoo, is revered by the staff of the company (Manjoo, 2018b).

Further, statistics that show a drop in Facebook users have other plausible explanations. Although a study by the Pew Research Center found that 26% of users deleted the Facebook app from their phones in 2018 (Perrin, 2018), it could be in response to widely reported research touting the benefits of taking breaks from social media (Fowler, 2017). Also, there is no evidence that these users deleted their Facebook accounts or are no longer accessing the platform via PC or by using a mobile browser on their phones.

The implementation of this disclaimer could also help to fend off regulatory actions by the legislative bodies of various countries, which are beginning to hold hearings to consider punitive policies toward social media platforms due to their roles in the spread of fake news. The disclaimer might even be seen as a proactive step on Wall Street and could prompt investors to express more confidence in the company. Also, since there is a new story almost every day about fake news on Facebook, it is safe to assume that most users know there is fake news on the platform, and Facebook's own research has proven that users will still share content tagged as false. If nothing else, a disclaimer will free us from the flood of stories about Facebook and their "fake news fix of the moment," since they would no longer have to come up with any. It would also help our information literacy efforts as librarians; seeing that disclaimer every time Facebook is opened would go a long way toward disestablishing it as an actual source of real news.

At one point or another, we've probably all been advised to count to 10 before expressing anger, or to write a letter airing a grievance but not to send it, or to "sleep on it" before making a major decision. Why can't these rules apply to social media? Short of the disclaimer button solution, another idea is to have a lag time before any links post. This would not affect status updates authored by the poster or personal photos, but any posted links would have to be vetted by the Facebook folks (one of the 20,000 human fact checkers and not the algorithm, since we have seen its limitations). There is an argument to be made that a delay violates the spirit of the organic conversations that Facebook intends to start and grow, but consider the simpler time of moderated electronic message boards. The board moderator had to physically read and approve any content before it was posted, and no one gave that a second thought. Also, Instagram, which is owned by Facebook, does not allow sharing of links at all, yet it has over 1 billion users and has remained largely fake news free (*The Economist*, 2018). Perhaps delayed gratification is the price we have to pay in order to stop fake news.

Another argument for a platform-generated pause button is the fact that "virality can cost lives," as evidenced by the fact that over 20 innocent people were lynched in India in 2018 after bogus charges of child abduction went viral on WhatsApp (*The Economist*, 2018). In response, WhatsApp (also owned by Facebook) implemented controls so that forwarded messages can only be sent to 20 people at a time; then in January 2019, they lowered that limit to five. Also, by eliminating their "quick forward" option, they essentially built their own pause button by adding an extra step into the WhatsApp process of sending content.

As librarians and information professionals, we have something that most corporations would do almost anything to obtain: a respected, trusted, widely known brand. Indeed, research by the Pew Internet Project found that 78% of American adults believe that libraries "help them find information that is trustworthy and reliable," with 56% stating that libraries help them "get information that helps with decisions they have to make" (Geiger, 2017). It is so heartening that people want to find quality information and believe that the library has the resources to help them to do so along with professional librarians who can best guide them in their use. The writing is on the wall – people are looking to us for help in finding high-quality sources of information and in evaluating its integrity and usefulness. Oftentimes, the challenge in meeting a goal lies in first figuring out what we want to achieve. In the realm of information, we know what we want to achieve – a world where facts triumph over falsehoods. Our users are looking to us to do this. It is critical that we rise to the occasion and meet and exceed their expectations. In doing so, we will be helping not only our users, but also the world at large.

To end this book, I would like to share a viewpoint that gives me great comfort. Writing in *Computers in Libraries*, Ben Johnson, Adult Services Manager of the Council Bluffs (Iowa) Public Library, offered this reminder: "Our communities support libraries because we are reputable and fair, not because we are the hottest and most exciting entertainment source. We must insist that we provide quality information, even if our communities choose not to use it. And if false information wins the day, we can take comfort in knowing that we kept the option of truth available. We made it theoretically possible for people to sort through the stories and get to the facts. We presented historical information that could have informed the discussion. And if the world ever gets tired of ignorant shouting matches, it will remember us. Through all of the mess, the library will emerge with its reputation intact. People will come back, not for ammunition to fight the information war, but to grow as individuals and as citizens" (Johnson, 2017).

# REFERENCES

Achenbach, J. (2018, May 25). Did the news media, led by Walter Cronkite, lose the war in Vietnam? *The Washington Post*. Retrieved from https://www.washingtonpost.com/national/did-the-news-media-led-by-walter-cronkite-lose-the-war-in-vietnam/2018/05/25/a5b3e098-495e-11e8-827e-190efaf1f1ee_story.html?noredirect=on&utm_term=.702160dc0c31.

Affelt, A. (2015). *The accidental data scientist: Big data applications and opportunities for librarians and information professionals.* Medford, NJ: Information Today, Inc.

Affelt, A. (2017). Fake news: The library imperative. In *Library and book trade almanac.* Medford, NJ: Information Today, Inc.

Allcott, H., Gentzkow, M., & Yu, C. (September 2018). *Trends in the diffusion of misinformation on social media.* Stanford, CA: Stanford Institute for Economic Policy Research. Retrieved from https://siepr.stanford.edu/system/files/publications/18-029.pdf.

Alvarez, B. (2017, January 11). Public libraries in the age of fake news. *Public Libraries Online.* Retrieved from http://publiclibrariesonline.org/2017/01/feature-public-libraries-in-the-age-of-fake-news/.

*American Libraries.* (2018, January/February). Libraries join the fight against fake news. *American Libraries.*

Atleo, S. (2013, November 4). Special bulletin on first nations education. *Assembly of First Nations*. Retrieved from http://www.afn.ca/2013/11/04/communique-from-the-national-chief-shawn-atleo-november-4-2013/.

Baer, D., & Lebowitz, S. (2015, October 19). 17 books Bill Gates thinks everyone should read. *Business Insider*. Retrieved from http://www.businessinsider.com/bill-gates-favorite-books-2015-10/#tap-dancing-to-work-warren-buffett-on-practically-everything-1966-2012-by-carol-loomis-1.

Banks, M. (2016, December 27). Fighting fake news: How libraries can lead the way on media literacy. *American Libraries*. Retrieved from https://americanlibrariesmagazine.org/2016/12/27/fighting-fake-news/.

Barringer, F., & Revkin, A. C. (2007, March 21). Gore warns congress of 'planetary emergency'. *The New York Times*. Retrieved from https://www.nytimes.com/2007/03/21/washington/21cnd-gore.html.

Blakeslee, S. (2004). The CRAAP test. *LOEX Quarterly*, *31*(3), Article 4. Retrieved from http://commons.emich.edu/loexquarterly/vol31/iss3/4.

Borchers, C. (2018, February 8). Twitter executive on fake news: We are not the arbiters of truth. *The Washington Post*. Retrieved from https://www.washingtonpost.com/news/the-fix/wp/2018/02/08/twitter-executive-on-fake-news-we-are-not-the-arbiters-of-truth/?utm_term=.2be26b37d3a3.

Borowitz, A. (2017a, January 22). Disturbed man gets past White House security, gives press conference. *The New Yorker*. Retrieved from https://www.newyorker.com/humor/borowitz-report/disturbed-man-gets-past-white-house-security-gives-press-conference.

Borowitz, A. (2017b, February 22). Americans overwhelmingly say lives have improved since Kellyanne Conway went away. *The New Yorker*. Retrieved from https://www.newyorker.com/humor/borowitz-report/americans-overwhelmingly-say-lives-have-improved-since-kellyanne-conway-went-away?mbid=social_facebook.

Brennan Center for Justice. (2017, January 31). *Debunking the voter fraud myth*. Retrieved from https://www.brennancenter.org/analysis/debunking-voter-fraud-myth.

BrightLocal. (2017). *Local consumer review survey*. Retrieved from https://www.brightlocal.com/learn/local-consumer-review-survey-2017/.

Broida, R. (2017, October 10). How to spot fake Amazon reviews. *CNET*. Retrieved from https://www.cnet.com/how-to/spot-fake-amazon-reviews-with-fakespot/.

Burgess, M. (2017, August 22). Silicon Valley can't handle hate. Should the state take over? *Wired*. Retrieved from http://www.wired.co.uk/article/hate-speech-online-fines-regulation-germany.

Burke, S. (2016, November 19). *Zuckerberg: Facebook will develop tools to fight fake news*. CNN. Retrieved from http://money.cnn.com/2016/11/19/technology/mark-zuckerberg-facebook-fake-news-election/index.html.

Calhoun, L. (2018, May 23). Just launched: Google news app uses artificial intelligence to select stories, stop fake news. *Inc.* Retrieved from https://www.inc.com/lisa-calhoun/new-google-news-app-uses-ai-to-select-stories-stop-fake-news.html.

Carey, B. (2018, January 1). Fake news: Wide reach but little impact, study suggests. *The New York Times*. Retrieved from https://www.nytimes.com/2018/01/02/health/fake-news-conservative-liberal.html.

Carlson, N. (2010, September 23). The Facebook movie is WRONG—Here's how much Zuckerberg actually gave the Winklevosses to go away. *Business Insider*. Retrieved from http://www.businessinsider.com/the-facebook-movie-is-wrong-heres-how-much-zuckerberg-actually-gave-the-winklevosses-to-go-away-2010-9.

Casad, B. J. (2016, August 1). Confirmation Bias. *Encyclopaedia Britannica*. Retrieved from https://www.britannica.com/science/confirmation-bias.

Cassino, D. (2016, November 9). Why pollsters were completely and utterly wrong. *Harvard Business Review*. Retrieved from https://hbr.org/2016/11/why-pollsters-were-completely-and-utterly-wrong.

CBC Radio. (2018a, August 17). *How a Canadian doctor's study on dandelion tea became fake news fodder*. CBC Radio White Coat Black Art. Retrieved from https://www.cbc.ca/radio/whitecoat/why-fake-news-is-bad-for-your-health-1.4423628/how-a-canadian-doctor-s-study-on-dandelion-tea-became-fake-news-fodder-1.4427348.

CBC Radio. (2018b, August 17). *News flash: Stem cells don't regrow your brain*. CBC Radio White Coat Black Art. Retrieved from https://www.cbc.ca/radio/whitecoat/why-fake-news-is-bad-for-your-health-1.4423628/news-flash-stem-cells-don-t-regrow-your-brain-1.4426301.

CBS News. (2017a, October 2). LAPD clarifies it cannot confirm Tom Petty's death. *CBS News*. Retrieved from https://www.cbsnews.com/news/lapd-clarifies-cannot-confirm-tompetty-death/.

CBS News. (2017b, August 2). Al Gore on why climate change is a national security threat. (2017, August 2). *CBS News*. Retrieved from https://www.cbsnews.com/news/

al-gore-climate-change-nationalsecurity-threat-an-inconvenient-sequel-truth-to-power/.

Chesney, R., & Citron, D. (2018, February 21). Deep fakes: A looming crisis for national security, democracy, and privacy? *Lawfare Blog*. Retrieved from https://www.lawfareblog.com/deep-fakes-looming-crisis-national-security-democracy-and-privacy.

Chesney, R., & Citron, D. K. (2019, forthcoming). Deep fakes: A looming challenge for privacy, democracy, and national security. *107 California Law Review*, p. 107.

Chokshi, N. (2017, April 26). That wasn't Mark Twain: How a misquotation is born. *The New York Times*. Retrieved from https://www.nytimes.com/2017/04/26/books/famous-misquotations.html.

CNN. (n.d.) *About CNN iReport*. Retrieved from http://ireport.cnn.com/about.jspa.

Constine, J. (2017, July 18). Facebook fights fake news spread via modified link previews. *TechCrunch*. Retrieved from https://techcrunch.com/2017/07/18/facebook-link-preview-modification/.

Crawford, K. (2018, September 14). *Study suggests Facebook's war on fake news is gaining ground*. Stanford, CA: Stanford Institute for Economic Policy Research. Retrieved from https://siepr.stanford.edu/news/facebook-fake-news-war?linkId=56984400.

de Castell, C. (2018, October 27). Email interview.

DePaulo, B., Ansfield, M. E., Kirkendol, S. E., & Boden, J. M. (2004). Serious lies. *Basic and Applied Social Psychology*, 26(2&3), 147–167.

DePaulo, B., Kashy, D. A., Kirkendol, S. E., Wyer, M. M., & Epstein, J. A. (1996). Lying in everyday life. *Journal of Personality and Social Psychology, 70*(5), 979–995.

Dewey, C. (2016, June 16). 6 in 10 of you will share this link without reading it, a new, depressing study says. *The Washington Post*. Retrieved from https://www.washingtonpost.com/news/the-intersect/wp/2016/06/16/six-in-10-of-you-will-share-this-link-without-reading-it-according-to-a-new-and-depressing-study/?utm_term=.a2cfd620f2c7.

Dillet, R. (2018, November 12). Facebook to let French regulators investigate on moderation processes. *TechCrunch*. Retrieved from https://techcrunch.com/2018/11/12/facebook-to-let-french-regulators-investigate-on-moderation-processes/.

DiResta, R. (2018, July 3). The complexity of simply searching for medical advice. *Wired*. Retrieved from https://www.wired.com/story/the-complexity-of-simply-searching-for-medical-advice/.

Domonoske, C. (2016, September 9). *After Facebook censored Iconic photo, Norwegian newspaper pushed back*. The Two-Way, National Public Radio. Retrieved from https://www.npr.org/sections/thetwo-way/2016/09/09/493267919/after-facebook-censors-iconic-photo-norwegian-newspaper-pushes-back.

Dwoskin, E. (2017, June 29). Twitter is looking for ways to let users flag fake news, offensive content. *The Washington Post*. Retrieved from https://www.washingtonpost.com/news/the-switch/wp/2017/06/29/twitter-is-looking-for-ways-to-let-users-flag-fake-news/?utm_term=.7abd18045f5f.

Edwards, J. (2015, April 27). The number of people actively using Twitter may be in decline. *Business Insider*. Retrieved from http://www.businessinsider.com/twitter-users-may-be-in-decline-2015-4.

eplettner. (2014, August 24). Fraud at the CDC uncovered, 340% risk of autism hidden from public. *CNN iReport.* Retrieved from http://ireport.cnn.com/docs/DOC-1164794.

Estepa, J. (2017, November 7). Trump has tweeted 2,461 times since the election. Here's a breakdown of his Twitter use. *USA Today.* Retrieved from https://www.usatoday.com/story/news/politics/onpolitics/2017/11/07/trump-has-tweeted-2-461-times-since-election-heres-breakdown-his-twitter-use/822312001/.

European Commission. (n.d.) Horizon 2020 website. Retrieved from https://ec.europa.eu/programmes/horizon2020/en/whathorizon-2020.

Facebook. (2018). *How do I mark a news story as false?* Retrieved from https://www.facebook.com/help/572838089565953.

Factcheck.org. (2018). *Our mission.* Retrieved from https://www.factcheck.org/about/our-mission/.

Fiegerman, S. (2016, November 17). *Facebook is well aware that it can influence elections.* CNN. Retrieved from http://money.cnn.com/2016/11/17/technology/facebook-election-influence/?iid=EL.

File, T. (2017, May 10). *Voting in America: A look at the 2016 presidential election.* Suitland, MD: United States Census Bureau. Retrieved from https://www.census.gov/newsroom/blogs/random-samplings/2017/05/voting_in_america.html.

Foer, F. (May 2018). The era of fake video begins. *The Atlantic.* Retrieved from https://www.theatlantic.com/magazine/archive/2018/05/realtys-end/556877.

Forster, K. (2017, January 7). Revealed: How dangerous fake health news conquered Facebook. *The Independent.* Retrieved from https://www.independent.co.uk/life-style/health-and-families/health-news/fake-news-health-facebook-cruel-damaging-social-media-mike-adams-natural-health-ranger-conspiracy-a7498201.html.

Fowler, G. A. (2017, February 1). Take back your brain from social media. *The Wall Street Journal.* Retrieved from https://www.wsj.com/articles/take-back-your-brain-from-social-media-1485968678.

Frenkel, S. (2018, June 28). Facebook and Twitter expand peek into who's behind their ads. *The New York Times.* Retrieved from https://www.nytimes.com/2018/06/28/technology/facebook-twitter-political-ads.html.

Frenkel, S., & Roose, K. (2018, April 25). Facebook's privacy scandal appears to have little effect on its bottom line. *The New York Times.* Retrieved from https://www.nytimes.com/2018/04/25/technology/facebook-privacy-earnings.html.

Gardiner, B. (2015, December 18). You'll be outraged at how easy it was to get you to click on this headline. *Wired.* Retrieved from https://www.wired.com/2015/12/psychology-of-clickbait/.

Gazaleh, A. (2018, September 27). Email interview.

Geiger, A. (2017, August 30). *Most Americans – Especially Millennials – Say libraries can help them find reliable, trustworthy information.* Washington, DC: Pew Research Center. Retrieved from http://www.pewresearch.org/fact-tank/2017/08/30/most-americans-especially-millennials-say-libraries-can-help-them-find-reliable-trustworthy-information/.

Ghosh, S. (2017, December 21). Facebook is scrapping its system of flagging fake news because it had 'the opposite effect of what we intended. *Business Insider*. Retrieved from http://www.businessinsider.com/facebook-drop-disputed-flags-fake-news-2017-12. Accessed on January 23, 2018.

Gingras, R. (2018, March 20). Elevating quality journalism on the open web. *Google Blog*. Retrieved from https://www.blog.google/outreach-initiatives/google-news-initiative/elevating-quality-journalism.

Glenza, J. (2018, August 23). Russian trolls 'spreading discord' over vaccine safety online. *The Guardian*. Retrieved from https://www.theguardian.com/society/2018/aug/23/russian-trolls-spread-vaccine-misinformation-on-twitter?CMP=edit_2221.

Gold, H. (2018, July 28). *UK 'fake news' report calls for tougher rules, fines for social media companies*. CNN. Retrieved from https://money.cnn.com/2018/07/28/media/uk-fake-news-report/index.html.

Goldman, J. (2016, October 17). 9 Insane statistics on the future of Internet video. *Inc*. Retrieved from https://www.inc.com/jeremy-goldman/9-insane-statistics-on-the-future-of-internet-video.html.

Greenwood, S., Perrin, A., & Duggan, M. (2016, November 11). *Social media update 2016*. Washington, DC: Pew Research Center. Retrieved from http://www.pewinternet.org/2016/11/11/social-media-update-2016/.

Griffith, E. (2017, October 12). Memo to Facebook: How to tell if you are a media company. *Wired*. Retrieved from https://www.wired.com/story/memo-to-facebook-how-to-tell-if-youre-a-media-company/.

Guess, A., Nyhan, B., & Reifler, J. (2018, January 9). *Selective exposure to misinformation: Evidence from the consumption of fake news during the 2016 U.S. presidential campaign.* European Research Council. Retrieved from http://www.dartmouth.edu/~nyhan/fake-news-2016.pdf.

Guidry, J. P. D., Carlyle, K., Messner, M., & Jin, Y. (2015). On pins and needles: How vaccines are portrayed on pinterest. *Vaccine, 33*(39), 5051–5056.

Gumberg Library, Duquesne University. (2018). *Information evaluation: The CRAAP test.* Retrieved from http://guides.library.duq.edu/informationevaluation/CRAAP.

Gyenes, N., & Mina, A. X. (2018, August 30). How misinfodemics spread disease. *The Atlantic.* Retrieved from https://www.theatlantic.com/technology/archive/2018/08/how-misinfodemics-spread-disease/568921/.

Hammond, C. (2017, February 9). How to spot misleading health news. *BBC Website.* Retrieved from http://www.bbc.com/future/story/20170207-how-to-spot-misleading-health-news.

Hatmaker, T. (2017, January 23). Bot-hunting Twitter bot sniffs out bogus political tweets. *TechCrunch.* Retrieved from https://techcrunch.com/2017/10/25/botometer-twitter-bot-hunting-probabot/.

Hawkins, D. (2018, July 31). The cybersecurity 202: Doctored videos could send fake news crisis into overdrive, lawmakers warn. *The Washington Post.* Retrieved from https://www.washingtonpost.com/news/powerpost/paloma/the-cybersecurity-202/2018/07/31/the-cybersecurity-202-doctored-videos-could-send-fake-news-crisis-into-overdrive-

lawmakers-warn/5b5f39c91b326b0207955e39/?utm_
term=.be54bb701fc9.

HealthNewsReview.org. (n.d.). *What we review and how.*
Retrieved from https://www.healthnewsreview.org/about-us/
how-we-rate-stories/.

Herrman, J. (2018, February 21). The making of a No. 1
YouTube conspiracy video after the Parkland tragedy. *The
New York Times*. Retrieved from https://www.nytimes.com/
2018/02/21/business/media/youtube-conspiracy-video-
parkland.html.

Holan, A. D. (2018, February 12). *The principles of the Truth-
O-Meter: PolitiFact's methodology for independent fact-
checking*. PolitiFact. Retrieved from https://www.politifact.
com/truth-o-meter/article/2018/feb/12/principles-truth-o-meter-
politifacts-methodology-i/#Truth-O-Meter%20ratings.

Horrigan, J. B. (2017, September 11). *The elements of the
information-engagement typology*. Washington, DC: Pew
Research Center. Retrieved from http://www.pewinternet.org/
2017/09/11/the-elements-of-the-information-engagement-
typology/.

Huff, D. (1954). *How to lie with statistics*. New York, NY:
W.W. Norton and Sons.

Hughes, T., Smith, J., & Leavitt, A. (2018, April 3). *Helping
people better assess the stories they see in newsfeed*. Facebook.
Retrieved from https://newsroom.fb.com/news/2018/04/news-
feed-fyi-more-context/.

Huppke, R. (2018a, March 13). Twitter post, 11:35 a.m.,
https://twitter.com/RexHuppke/status/973598388649414658.

Huppke, R. (2018b, November 8). Absured Acosta story
shows how disinformation bubbles from bots to the White

House. *The Chicago Tribune*. Retrieved from https://
www.chicagotribune.com/news/opinion/huppke/ct-met-
acosta-video-white-house-chop-intern-huppke-20181108-
story.html?fbclid=IwAR1szYk0uhkAm21fo1WUD4FAe6v
Q2Co7Nlklmo3ELz0ayp5NIWQ4xU3NzQQ.

IFLA. (2017, February 1). *How to spot fake news—IFLA in
the post-truth society*. The Hague, Netherlands: International
Federation of Library Associations and Institutions. Retrieved
from https://www.ifla.org/node/11175.

IFLA Website. (2017, March 1). *CNN broadcasts how to spot
fake news infographic*. The Hague, Netherlands: International
Federation of Library Associations and Institutions. Retrieved
from https://www.ifla.org/ES/node/11236.

IMDb. (n.d.). *The Social Network*. Retrieved from
https://www.imdb.com/title/tt1285016/characters/nm
0005493.

InVID Verification Plugin. (2018). Retrieved from https://
www.invid-project.eu/tools-and-services/invid-verification-
plugin/.

Irwin, N. (2017, January 18). Researchers created fake
news. Here's what they found. *The New York Times*.
Retrieved from https://www.nytimes.com/2017/01/18/upshot/
researchers-created-fake-news-heres-what-they-found.html.

Jacobson, T. (2018, October 23). Email communication.

Jacoby, J. (Writer, Director, & Producer), & Bourg, A.
(Writer). (2018). The Facebook dilemma. In R. Aronson-
Rath, K. Druckerman, D. Fanning, B. Tarver, (Executive
producers), *Frontline*. Boston, MA: WGBH.

Jenkins, A. (2018, April 6). *We're keeping track of all of
Facebook's scandals so you don't have to. Fortune*. Retrieved

from http://fortune.com/2018/04/06/facebook-scandals-mark-zuckerberg/.

Johnson, B. (2017). Information literacy is dead: The role of libraries in a post-truth world. *Computers in Libraries, 37*(2), 12–15.

Johnson, T. (2018, June 28). *Are your eyes lying to you? Experts, Pentagon hunt for tools to detect Hoax videos.* McClatchy Washington Bureau. Retrieved from https://www.mcclatchydc.com/news/nation-world/national/national-security/article213987384.html.

Jones, T. (2007, December 19). Dewey defeats Truman. *The Chicago Tribune.* Retrieved from http://www.chicagotribune.com/news/nationworld/politics/chi-chicagodays-deweydefeats-story-story.html.

Kan, M. (2018, January 2). Facebook was biggest distributor of fake news, study finds. *PC Magazine.* Retrieved from https://www.pcmag.com/news/358248/study-finds-facebook-was-the-biggest-distributor-of-fake-new.

Kantrowitz, A. (2016, April 26). As social shifts to video, content creators win power and dollars. *BuzzFeed News.* Retrieved from https://www.buzzfeed.com/alexkantrowitz/as-social-shifts-to-video-content-creators-win-power-and-dol?utm_term=.oomrD2vPkR#.ykmokrMg8E.

Kelly, M. (2018, November 12). Facebook will allow French regulators to monitor content moderation processes. *The Verge.* Retrieved from https://www.theverge.com/2018/11/12/18089012/facebook-france-emmanuel-macron-hate-speech?nr_email_referer=1&pt=385758&ct=Sailthru_BI_Newsletters&mt=8.

Kelly, M. L. (2018, April 11). *Media or tech company? Facebook's profile is blurry.* National Public Radio. Retrieved from https://www.npr.org/2018/04/11/601560213/media-or-tech-company-facebooks-profile-is-blurry.

Kent State University Libraries. (2018). *Online satirical news: List of satirical news sites.* Kent, OH: Kent State University Libraries. Retrieved from https://libguides.library.kent.edu/c.php?g5278400&p51854632.

Kessler, G. (2013, September 11). *About the fact checker.* Retrieved from https://www.washingtonpost.com/news/fact-checker/about-the-fact-checker/?utm_term=.c2a16a b22489.

Knight, W. (2018a, July 18). How to tell if you're talking to a bot. *MIT Technology Review.* Retrieved from https://www.technologyreview.com/s/611655/how-to-tell-if-youre-talking-to-a-bot/.

Knight, W. (2018b, August 17). Fake America great again. *MIT Technology Review.* Retrieved from https://www.technology review.com/s/611810/fake-america-great-again.

Kokalitcheva, K. (2016, November 11). Mark Zuckerberg says fake news on Facebook affecting the election is a 'crazy idea'. *Fortune.* Retrieved from http://fortune.com/2016/11/11/facebook-election-fake-news-mark-zuckerberg/.

Kosslyn, J., & Yu, C. (2017, April 7). Fact check now available in Google search and news around the world. *Google Blog.* Retrieved from https://www.blog.google/products/search/fact-check-now-available-google-search-and-news-around-world/.

Kot, F. C., & Jones, J. L. (2015). The impact of library resource utilization on undergraduate students' academic performance: A propensity score matching design. *College and Research Libraries, 76*(5), 566–586.

Kurtz, H. (2003, March 20). A permanent exclusive. *The Washington Post*. Retrieved from https://www.washingtonpost.com/archive/business/technology/2003/03/20/a-permanent-exclusive/e1027609-669e-42b4-9fe2-7cc09f931ea5/?utm_term=.f76ef9407f2b. Accessed on March 8, 2018.

Lapowsky, I. (2018, August 20). This browser extension is like an antivirus for fake photos. *Wired*. Retrieved from https://www.wired.com/story/surfsafe-browser-extension-save-you-from-fake-photos/.

Lasda, E. (2018, October 18). Email interview.

Lazer, D. M., Baum, M. A., Benkler, Y., Berinsky, A. J., Greenhill, K. M., Menczer, F. (2018). The science of fake news. *Science*, *359*(6380), 1094–1096.

Levin, S. (2018, July 3). Is Facebook a publisher? In public it says no, but in court it says yes. *The Guardian*. Retrieved from https://www.theguardian.com/technology/2018/jul/02/facebook-mark-zuckerberg-platform-publisher-lawsuit?CMP=share_btn_tw.

*Library Journal*. (2017, June 6–20). Fighting fake news. *Library Journal*. Retrieved from https://learn.libraryjournal.com/courses/fighting-fake-news/.

Lin, H. (2018, February 27). The danger of deep fakes: Responding to Bobby Chesney and Danielle Citron. *Lawfare Blog*. Retrieved from https://www.lawfareblog.com/danger-deep-fakes-responding-bobby-chesney-and-danielle-citron.

Lohr, S., & Singer, N. (2016, November 10). How data failed us in calling an election. *The New York Times*. Retrieved from https://www.nytimes.com/2016/11/10/technology/the-data-said-clinton-would-win-why-you-shouldnt-have-believed-it.html.

Lueck, T. (2004, October 17). Pierre Salinger, Kennedy Aide, Dies at 79. *The New York Times*. Retrieved from https://www.nytimes.com/2004/10/17/politics/pierre-salinger-kennedy-aide-dies-at-79.html.

Lupkin, S. (2014, October 9). How a now-retracted autism study went viral – again. *ABC News*. Retrieved from https://abcnews.go.com/Health/now-retracted-autism-study-viral/story?id=25248179.

Lyons, T. (2017, December 20). News feed FYI: Replacing disputed flags with related articles. *Facebook Blog*. Retrieved from https://newsroom.fb.com/news/2017/12/news-feed-fyi-updates-in-our-fight-against-misinformation/.

Maack, M. M. (2017, July 7). *EU funded InVID launches a fake video news debunker*. The Next Web. Retrieved from https://thenextweb.com/eu/2017/07/07/eu-funded-invid-launches-fake-video-news-debunker/.

Mack, D. (2018, April 17). This PSA about fake news from Barack Obama is not what it appears. *BuzzFeed*. Retrieved from https://www.buzzfeednews.com/article/davidmack/obama-fake-news-jordan-peele-psa-video-buzzfeed.

Manjoo, F., & Roose, K. (2017, October 31). How to fix Facebook? We asked 9 experts. *The New York Times*. Retrieved from https://www.nytimes.com/2017/10/31/technology/how-to-fix-facebook-we-asked-9-experts.html.

Manjoo, F. (2018a, August 1). Stumbles? What stumbles? Big tech is as strong as ever. *The New York Times*. Retrieved from https://www.nytimes.com/2018/08/01/technology/big-tech-earnings-stumbles.html?rref=collection%2Fissuecollection%2Ftodays-new-york-times&action=click&content Collection=todayspaper&region=rank&module=package&version=highlights&contentPlacement=3&pgtype=collection.

Manjoo, F. (2018b, November 1). How Mark Zuckerberg became too big to fail. *The New York Times*. Retrieved from https://www.nytimes.com/2018/11/01/technology/mark-zuckerberg-facebook.html.

Martinez, A. G. (2018, March 26). The blockchain solution to our deepfake problems. *Wired*. Retrieved from https://www.wired.com/story/the-blockchain-solution-to-our-deepfake-problems/.

Matsakis, L. (2018, February 14). Artificial intelligence is now fighting fake porn. *Wired*. Retrieved from https://www.wired.com/story/gfycat-artificial-intelligence-deepfakes/.

Merriam-Webster. (n.d.). *Definition of metadata*. Retrieved from https://www.merriam-webster.com/dictionary/metadata.

Metaliteracy. (n.d.) Metaliteracy Badging System. Retrieved from https://metaliteracy.org/ml-in-practice/metaliteracy-badging/.

Meyer, R. (2018, March 8). The grim conclusions of the largest-ever study of fake news. *The Atlantic*. Retrieved from https://www.theatlantic.com/technology/archive/2018/03/largest-study-ever-fake-news-mit-twitter/555104/.

Michigan Library Research Guides. (2018). *Fake news, lies and propaganda: How to sort fact from fiction*. Retrieved from http://guides.lib.umich.edu/fakenews.

*Michigan News*. (2017, February 16). U-M Library Battles Fake News with New Class. *Michigan News*. Retrieved from http://ns.umich.edu/new/releases/24593-u-m-library-battles-fakenews-with-new-class.

Miller, M. (2017, July 18). Watch this video of Obama – It's the future of fake news. *Fast Company*. Retrieved from https://

www.fastcompany.com/90133566/watch-this-video-an-ai-created-of-obama-its-the-future-of-fake-news.

Mis-Quotations. (n.d.) *The Walden Woods Project*. Retrieved from https://www.walden.org/thoreau/mis-quotations/.

MIT Sloan School of Management. (2018, March 8). *Study: False news spreads faster than the truth*. Retrieved from http://mitsloan.mit.edu/newsroom/articles/study-false-news-spreads-faster-than-the-truth/.

Mitchell, A., Gottfried, J., & Matsa, K. E. (2015, June 1). *Millennials and political news*. Washington, DC: Pew Research Center. Retrieved from http://www.journalism.org/2015/06/01/millennials-political-news/.

Mitchell, A., Barthel, M., Holcomb, J., & Weisel, R. (2016, December 15). *Many Americans believe fake news is sowing confusion*. Washington, DC: Pew Research Center. Retrieved from http://www.journalism.org/2016/12/15/many-americans-believe-fake-news-is-sowing-confusion/.

Morris, C. (2018, April 25). Twitter and the Trump effect: Tracking the mobile user numbers. *Fortune*. Retrieved from http://fortune.com/2018/04/25/twitter-trump-effect-user-numbers/.

National Health Service. *Behind the headlines: Your guide to science that makes sense*. Retrieved from https://www.nhs.uk/news/.

National Public Radio. (2016, December 14). Fake news expert on how false stories spread and why people believe them. *Fresh Air*. https://www.npr.org/2016/12/14/505547295/fake-news-expert-onhow-false-stories-spread-and-why-people-believe-them.

National Public Radio. (2018, July 17). *Transcript: Obama's speech at the 2018 Nelson Mandela Annual Lecture.* Retrieved from https://www.npr.org/2018/07/17/629862434/ transcript-obamas-speech-at-the-2018-nelson-mandela-annual-lecture.

Nicas, J. (2018, July 7). Oprah, is that you? On social media, the answer is often no. *The New York Times.* Retrieved from https://www.nytimes.com/2018/07/07/technology/facebook-instagram-twitter-celebrity-impostors.html.

Nott, G. (2018, June 14). Obama tech advisor: Fun's over for AI-driven 'deep fake' video. *Computerworld Australia.* Retrieved from https://www.computerworld.com.au/article/ 642424/obama-tech-advisor-fun-over-ai-driven-deep-fake-video.

O'Brien, K. (2018, October 18). Email interview.

Ojala, M. (2017). Fake business news. *Online Searcher, 41*(3), 60–62.

Pariser, E. (2012). *The filter bubble: What the Internet is hiding from you.* New York, NY: Penguin Press.

Perlberg, S., & Seetharaman, D. (2016, June 22). Facebook signs deal with media companies, celebrities for Facebook live. *The Wall Street Journal.* Retrieved from https:// www.wsj.com/articles/facebook-signs-deals-with-media-companies-celebrities-for-facebook-live-1466533472.

Perrin, A. (2018, September 5). *Americans are changing their relationship with Facebook.* Washington, DC: Pew Research Center. Retrieved from http://www.pewresearch.org/fact-tank/2018/09/05/americans-are-changing-their-relationship-with-facebook/

Pierson, D. (2018, February 19). Fake videos are on the rise. As they become more realistic, seeing shouldn't always be believing. *The Los Angeles Times*. Retrieved from http://www.latimes.com/business/technology/la-fi-tn-fake-videos-20180219-story.html

Price, R. (2016, November 17). A report that fake news 'outperformed' real news on Facebook suggests the problem is wildly out of control. *Business Insider*. Retrieved from http://www.businessinsider.com/fake-news-outperformed-real-news-on-facebook-before-us-election-report-2016-11

ProQuest. (2016). *Toward an Information Literate Society*. Retrieved from https://media2.proquest.com/documents/surveyresults-informationliteracy-2016.pdf.

Reid, J. (2006, July 17). *'Pierre Salinger Syndrome' and the TWA 800 conspiracies*. CNN. Retrieved from http://www.cnn.com/2006/US/07/12/twa.conspiracy/.

Resnick, B. (2018, July 24). We're underestimating the mind-warping potential of fake video. *Vox*. Retrieved from https://www.vox.com/science-and-health/2018/4/20/17109764/deepfake-ai-false-memory-psychology-mandela-effect.

Reuters.com. (2017, January 31). *Covering Trump the Reuters way*. Retrieved from https://www.reuters.com/article/rpb-adlertrump-idUSKBN15F276.

Robbins, N. (2012, August 4). Another misleading graph of Romney's tax plan. *Forbes*. Retrieved from https://www.forbes.com/sites/naomirobbins/2012/08/04/another-misleading-graph-of-romneys-tax-plan/#59bcbc7033b8

Roose, K. (2017, October 2). After Las Vegas shooting, fake news regains its megaphone. *The New York Times*. Retrieved from https://www.nytimes.com/2017/10/02/business/las-vegas-shooting-fake-news.html.

Roose, K. (2018, November 7). Facebook Thwarted Chaos on election day. It's hardly clear that will last. *The New York Times*. Retrieved from https://www.nytimes.com/2018/11/07/business/facebook-midterms-misinformation.html.

Roose, K. (2018, November 5). 6 types of misinformation to beware of on election day. *The New York Times*. Retrieved from https://www.nytimes.com/2018/11/05/us/politics/misinformation-election-day.html.

Rothman, J. (2018, November 12). In the age of A.I., is seeing still believing? *The New Yorker*. Retrieved from https://www.newyorker.com/magazine/2018/11/12/in-the-age-of-ai-is-seeing-still-believing.

Sanders, S. (2017, June 20). *Upworthy was one of the hottest sites ever. You won't believe what happened next.* National Public Radio. Retrieved from https://www.npr.org/sections/alltechconsidered/2017/06/20/533529538/upworthy-was-one-of-the-hottest-sites-ever-you-wont-believe-what-happened-next.

Sandler, R. (2018a, July 6). Facebook has apologized after flagging parts of the declaration of independence as hate speech. *Business Insider*. Retrieved from http://www.businessinsider.com/facebook-declaration-of-independence-hate-speech-2018-7.

Sandler, R. (2018b, July 18). People are really upset over Mark Zuckerberg's refusal to Ban Holocaust Deniers from Facebook. *Business Insider*. Retrieved from http://www.businessinsider.com/mark-zuckerberg-facebook-holocaust-deniers-reaction-2018.

Schmidt, S., & Phillips, K. (2018, June 22). The crying Honduran girl on the cover of time was not separated from her mother. *The Washington Post*. Retrieved from https://

www.washingtonpost.com/news/morning-mix/wp/2018/06/
22/the-crying-honduran-girl-on-the-cover-of-time-was-not-
separated-from-her-mother-father-says/?utm_term=.
15d6be62e437.

Seetharaman, D. (2018, January 19). Facebook to rank news
sources by quality to battle misinformation. *The Wall Street
Journal*. Retrieved from https://www.wsj.com/articles/
facebook-to-rank-news-sources-by-quality-to-battle-
misinformation-1516394184.

Segreti, G. (2016, August 29). Facebook CEO says group will
not become a media company. *Reuters*. Retrieved from https://
uk.reuters.com/article/us-facebook-zuckerberg-
idUKKCN1141WN.

Shahani, A. (2016, November 17). *From hate speech to fake
news: The content crisis facing Mark Zuckerberg*. National
Public Radio. Retrieved from https://www.npr.org/sections/
alltechconsidered/2016/11/17/495827410/from-hate-speech-
to-fake-news-the-content-crisis-facing-mark-zuckerberg.

Shearer, E., & Gottfried, J. (2017, September 7). *News use
across social media platforms 2017*. Washington, DC: Pew
Research Center. Retrieved from http://www.journalism.org/
2017/09/07/news-use-across-social-media-platforms-
2017/.

Shere, D. (2012, July 31). *Dishonest fox chart: Bush tax cut
edition*. Media Matters for America. Retrieved from https://
www.mediamatters.org/blog/2012/07/31/dishonest-fox-chart-
bush-tax-cut-edition/189046.

Shuessler, J. (2018, October 4). Hoaxers slip breastaurants
and dog-park sex into journals. *The New York Times*.
Retrieved from https://www.nytimes.com/2018/10/04/arts/
academic-journals-hoax.html.

Silverman, C. (2016, November 16). This analysis shows how viral fake election news stories outperformed real news on Facebook. *BuzzFeed*. Retrieved from https://www.buzzfeed.com/craigsilverman/viral-fake-election-news-outperformed-real-news-on-facebook?utm_term=.rtEzOb0BN#.gs1vP X1QD.

Silverman, C. (2018, April 17). How to spot a deepfake like the Barack Obama-Jordan Peele video. *BuzzFeed*. Retrieved from https://www.buzzfeed.com/craigsilverman/obama-jordan-peele-deepfake-video-debunk-buzzfeed?utm_term=.uyYKWN8mk#.bhzKX7rlp.

Snopes.com. *About us*. Retrieved from https://www.snopes.com/about-snopes/.

Solon, O. (2016, November 10). Facebook's failure: Did fake news and polarized politics get Trump elected? *The Guardian*. Retrieved from https://www.theguardian.com/technology/2016/nov/10/facebook-fake-news-election-conspiracy-theories.

Sonderman, J. (2011, July 19). 5 reasons people share news and how you can get them to share yours. *Poynter Institute*. Retrieved from https://www.poynter.org/news/5-reasons-people-share-news-how-you-can-get-them-share-yours.

Special Libraries Association. (2016, April 13). *Competencies for Information Professionals*. Retrieved from https://www.sla.org/about-sla/competencies/.

Statista. (2018). *Share of search queries handled by leading U.S. search engine providers as of April 2018*. Retrieved from https://www.statista.com/statistics/267161/market-share-of-search-engines-in-the-united-states/.

Statista. (2018). *Number of monthly active Facebook users worldwide*. Retrieved from https://www.statista.com/

statistics/264810/number-of-monthly-active-facebook-users-worldwide/.

Statista. (2018). *Percentage of U.S. adults who use Twitter as of January 2018, by age group*. Retrieved from https://www.statista.com/statistics/265647/share-of-us-internet-users-who-use-twitter-by-age-group/.

Statista. (2018). *Share of adults who believe fake news is a major problem in the United States in 2017, by political affiliation*. Retrieved from https://www.statista.com/statistics/657074/fake-news-confusion-level-by-political-affiliation/.

Stein, S. (2017, October 2). Google ends search-result punishment for news behind paywalls. *CNET*. Retrieved from https://www.cnet.com/news/google-ends-paywall-punishment-for-news-search/.

Steinmetz, K. (2018, August 9). How your brain tricks you into believing fake news. *Time*. Retrieved from http://time.com/5362183/the-real-fake-news-crisis/.

Stewart, E. (2016, June 8). Election 2016 will make or break Twitter: Here's how the struggling social network plans to win. *TheStreet*. Retrieved from https://www.thestreet.com/story/13587479/1/election-2016-will-make-or-break-twitter-here-s-how-the-struggling-social-network-plans-to-win.html.

Sullivan, B. T., & Porter, K. L. (2016). From one-shot sessions to embedded librarian: Lessons learned over seven years of successful faculty-librarian collaboration. *College and Research Libraries News*, *77*(1), 34–37.

Sullivan, M. (2018, July 17). Facebook can never stop fake news, and still be Facebook. *Fast Company*. Retrieved from https://www.fastcompany.com/90203347/facebook-can-never-stop-fake-news-and-still-be-facebook.

Terdiman, D. (2018, January 19). Can we trust Facebook's users to determine what news we should trust? *Fast Company*. Retrieved from https://www.fastcompany.com/40519310/facebook-to-survey-users-about-trustworthy-news-sources.

The American Library Association. (n.d). *Information literacy competency standards for higher education*. Retrieved from http://www.ala.org/Template.cfm?Section=Home& template=/ContentManagement/ContentDisplay.cfm& ContentID=33553.

*The Economist*. (2017a, November 4). Once considered a boon to democracy, social media have started to look like its nemesis. *The Economist*. Retrieved from https://www.economist.com/briefing/2017/11/04/once-considered-a-boon-to-democracy-social-media-have-started-to-look-like-its-nemesis.

*The Economist*. (2017b, July 1). Fake news: You ain't seen nothing yet. *The Economist*. Retrieved from https://www.economist.com/science-and-technology/2017/07/01/fake-news-you-aint-seen-nothing-yet.

*The Economist*. (2018, July 26). WhatsApp suggests a cure for virality. *The Economist*. Retrieved from https://www.economist.com/leaders/2018/07/26/whatsapp-suggests-a-cure-for-virality.

The Editors of Encyclopaedia Britannica. (n.d.) *Walter Cronkite*. Encyclopaedia Britannica. Retrieved from https://www.britannica.com/biography/Walter-Cronkite.

The State Library of Iowa. (n.d.). *Steps of the Reference Interview*. Iowa Library Services Information Literacy Toolkit. Retrieved from https://www.statelibraryofiowa.org/ld/i-j/infolit/toolkit/geninfo/refinterview.

The Trust Project. (2017a). *Frequently asked questions.* Retrieved from https://thetrustproject.org/faq/#indicator.

The Trust Project. (2017b). *Who we are.* Retrieved from https://thetrustproject.org/.

Thompson, M. S. (2013, April 10). Melding the nitty gritty of critical thinking and information literacy into English developmental and composition classes. Paper presented at ACRL conference, April 10–13, 2013, Indianapolis, Indiana. Retrieved from http://www.ala.org/acrl/sites/ala.org.acrl/files/content/conferences/confsandpreconfs/2013/papers/Thompson_Melding.pdf.

Thornburg, R. M. (2011). *Producing online news: Digital skills, stronger stories* (p. 85). Washington, DC: CQ Press.

Tiffany, K. (2017, March 17). In 2010, the social network was searing—Now it looks quaint. *The Verge.* Retrieved from https://www.theverge.com/2017/3/17/14946570/the-social-network-facebook-mark-zuckerberg-president-of-the-world.

Tiku, N. (2018, March 19). Europe's new privacy law will change the web and more. *Wired.* Retrieved from https://www.wired.com/story/europes-new-privacy-law-will-change-the-web-and-more/.

Timberg, C., & Dwoskin, E. (2018, July 6). Twitter is sweeping out fake accounts like never before, putting user growth at risk. *The Washington Post.* Retrieved from https://www.washingtonpost.com/technology/2018/07/06/twitter-is-sweeping-out-fake-accounts-like-never-before-putting-user-growth-risk/?utm_term=.6583564b1f65.

Tufekci, Z. (2016, November 15). Mark Zuckerberg is in Denial. *The New York Times.* Retrieved from https://www.nytimes.com/2016/11/15/opinion/mark-zuckerberg-is-in-denial.html?_r=1.

Valenza, J. (2016, November 26). Truth, truthiness, triangulation: A news literacy toolkit for a 'Post-Truth' world. *School Library Journal*. Retrieved from http://blogs.slj.com/neverendingsearch/2016/11/26/truth-truthiness-triangulation-and-the-librarian-way-a-news-literacy-toolkit-for-a-post-truth-world/.

Valenza, J. (2018, March 14). Telephone interview.

Vivalt, E. (2018, July 27). How to be a smart consumer of social science research. *Harvard Business Review*. Retrieved from https://hbr.org/2018/07/how-to-be-a-smart-consumer-of-social-science-research?utm_medium=email&utm_source=newsletter_daily&utm_campaign=mtod_not_activesubs&referral=00203&deliveryName=DM15984.

Vosoughi, S., Roy, D., & Aral, S. (2018). The spread of true and false news online. *Science, 359*, 1146–1151.

Wang, V. (2017, December 2). ABC suspends Brian Ross over erroneous report about Trump. *The New York Times*. Retrieved from https://www.nytimes.com/2017/12/02/us/brian-ross-suspended-abc.html.

Wang, S. (2018, June 26). Twitter ramps up fight against abuse and malicious bots. *Bloomberg*. Retrieved from https://www.bloomberg.com/news/articles/2018-06-26/twitter-ramps-up-fight-against-abuse-and-malicious-bots.

Wardle, C. (2017, February 16). Fake news. Its complicated. *First Draft*. Retrieved from https://firstdraftnews.org/fake-news-complicated/.

Wardle, C. (July 2018). Information disorder: The essential glossary. *First Draft*. Retrieved from https://firstdraftnews.org/wp-content/uploads/2018/07/infoDisorder_glossary.pdf?x30563.

Weinberger, M. (2018, May 14). Mark Zuckerberg just turned 34 years old. Here are 33 photos of Facebook's rise from a Harvard Dorm Room to world domination. *Business Insider*. Retrieved from http://www.businessinsider.com/facebook-history-photos-2016-9.

Wells, T. (2008, November 16). Onion nation: A look inside the offices of the onion. *The Washington Post*. Retrieved from http://www.washingtonpost.com/wp-dyn/content/article/2008/11/07/AR2008110701942_pf.html.

Woollaston, V. (2017, January 11). *Facebook's journalism project wants to finally crack the problem of fake news.* Retrieved from http://www.wired.co.uk/article/facebook-journalism-tools.

Zelizer, J. (2017, July 19). *Did the Rodney King video change anything?* CNN. Retrieved from https://www.cnn.com/2017/07/19/opinions/zelizer-nineties-rodney-king-video/index.html.

Zillman, C. (2016, June 14). Why Facebook could be 'all video' in five years. *Fortune*. Retrieved from http://fortune.com/2016/06/14/facebook-video-live/.

Zimdars, M. (2016a). *False, Misleading, Clickbait-y, and Satirical 'News' Sources.* Retrieved from https://docs.google.com/document/d/10eA5-mCZLSS4MQY5QGb5ewC3VAL6pLkT53V_81ZyitM/preview.

Zimdars, M. (2016b, November 18). My 'fake-news' list went viral. But made-up stories are only part of the problem. *The Washington Post*. Retrieved from https://www.washingtonpost.com/posteverything/wp/2016/11/18/my-fake-news-list-went-viral-but-made-up-stories-are-only-part-of-the-problem/?utm_term=.a9def4fed318.

# ABOUT THE AUTHOR

Photo by Michael G. Leslie

Amy Affelt has spent her entire career in economic consulting, where she finds, analyses, and transforms information and data into knowledge deliverables for PhD economists who testify as experts in litigation. She is a frequent writer and conference speaker on fake news, Big Data, Internet of Things, adding value to information, evaluating information integrity and quality, and marketing information services. She is the author of a book, *The Accidental Data*

*Scientist: Big Data Applications and Opportunities for Librarians and Information Professionals* (Information Today, 2015), and is the Big Data columnist for *EContent* magazine. She has a BA in History, Phi Beta Kappa, from the University of Illinois at Chicago and a Master's degree in Library and Information Science from Dominican University. She is a Fellow of the Special Libraries Association.

# INDEX

Printed in the United States
By Bookmasters